LED ZEPPELIN

IN THE LIGHT 1968–1980

If Elvis Presley and Little Richard dominated the 50s, and The Beatles and The Rolling Stones dominated the 60s, Led Zeppelin, the biggest-selling rock group the world has ever known, have unarguably dominated the 70s.

IN THE LIGHT is the first fully-comprehensive large format book to document the group's meteoric rise and their years at the top. It draws on ten years of extensive research, and traces items from world-wide sources, many never seen outside their country of origin. It starts with the band's humble beginnings, and provides considerable pictorial and written coverage of the main events of the Zeppelin era such as the early solo careers, The Yardbirds, The New Yardbirds, Zeppelin's conquest of America, subsequent fan interest in the band's home country, the band's tours and recordings, their film and their album sleeve designs, their important decision to add spectacle to their stage presentation, their musical conquests of Europe and other countries, as well as their triumphs gathering awards and prizes.

Quotes from individual Zeppelin members and from the press provide additional insight into the band and their music. Special attention is paid to John Bonham.

But IN THE LIGHT is more than just another music book. It is what its authors feel the group's true fans would prefer — an honest record of Led Zeppelin rather than the opportunist, sensationalized approach to 'documentation' that has so angered the group and their management in the past.

The authors' total commitment and genuine admiration for Led Zeppelin and a music which ranges from powerful leviathan rock to a softer, wistful, melodic side, is apparent throughout their book, which in its detail, scope and intent, stands as a testament to the group's music during their incredible 12 years as a band.

It is a book which the Led Zeppelin fan will be proud to own.

1

AUTHORS' DEDICATION

The size and devotion of the following that Led Zeppelin have built has been rivalled by few bands during their career. Their musical field covered a diverse range of material, but they followed no fashion or trends; instead they made their own rules and set a constant high standard that few could match.

Each member of the band was an integral part of the musical formula they developed, and it seems hard to accept that the pleasure and musical intensity of the group in full flight onstage will not be felt again.

Led Zeppelin were genuinely loved by their audiences, to whom they gave such warmth with their friendly rapport and good humor. This book is dedicated to them, and especially to the memory of John Bonham.

Titles in the PROTEUS ROCKS series:

PROTEUS BOOKS is an imprint of The Proteus Publishing Group

United States
PROTEUS PUBLISHING CO., INC.
733 Third Avenue, New York, N.Y. 10017
Distributed by
THE SCRIBNER BOOK COMPANIES, INC.
597 Fifth Avenue, New York, N.Y. 10017

United Kingdom
PROTEUS (PUBLISHING) LIMITED
Bremar House, Sale Place, London W2 1PT

© **1981 Savoy Editions Ltd**
Text © 1981 Howard Mylett
All rights reserved

ISBN 0 906071 25 9

Printed and bound in Italy by New Interlitho S.P.A., Milan

Artwork by Classic Publications, Manchester.

LED ZEPPELIN

IN THE LIGHT
1968–1980

**RICHARD BUNTON
&
HOWARD MYLETT**

A SAVOY EDITIONS BOOK
PROTEUS
London & New York

EARLY HISTORY

Jimmy Page joined his first group, Neil Christian and the Crusaders, upon leaving school. He was a keen record collector, and studied the styles of 1950s guitar players Scotty Moore and James Burton, who played on records cut by Elvis Presley and Ricky Nelson.

During Jimmy's spell with the band, Neil Christian developed a keen interest in Bo Diddley and Chuck Berry and lesser known rhythm'n'blues singers, on whom they based some of their music.

Glandular fever forced Jimmy to leave Neil Christian and return to art school where he played guitar with Cyril Davies' All Stars. He was eventually approached to play session work, a field which allowed him to be inventive and imaginative on guitar and to develop a wide range of styles from ambitious solos to orchestral. He was given work with big bands such as Burt Bacharach's and Johnny Dankworth's.

His first two sessions, on Jet Harris's and Tony Meehan's *Diamonds* and Carter Lewis's *Your Momma's Out of Town*, caused considerable interest, and he quickly became a top session man; his anonymity allowed even well established groups to employ his services, and during the period 1963-

Top: *Circa 1963. Carter Lewis and the
Southerners (Jimmy Page extreme right).
Promotion photo. "Your Momma's out of
Town"/"Somebody Told my Girl"
(ORIOLE 1868).*
Middle: *"The Band of Joy"*
Bottom: *Circa 1964. John Paul Jones
during session days.*

1965 he was *the* session man.

Simultaneously, he was experimenting with fuzz box, distortion and feedback, and did some incredibly fast solos, developing an easily distinguishable style of his own; he was also still being presented with written arrangements to work from.

He sometimes 'mimicked' revamped forms of the 1950s, mainly American rock'n'roll guitar solos for the instrumental passages of records by solo artists of the 1960s.

He worked with Shel Talmy, producer of The Kinks and The Who, and was prominently featured on other Talmy produced groups.

Top: Circa 1964. Mickey Finn and the Bluemen (Jimmy Page extreme left). "I played mouth organ and lead guitar with them for a while." Promotion photo.
Bottom: Sept. 1967. Robert Plant publicity shot for C.B.S. Records.

Sometimes his role was to enrich the sound of the band he worked for, although several solos of his were slotted in on some of the tracks.

He was selected for

Andrew Loog Oldham's *Immediate* label to work as an A&R man and producer, and occasionally co-writer, as well as player (notably with Eric Clapton on some tracks). In later

years some rehearsal tracks solely featuring Eric and Jimmy were issued by the label, to cash in on the duo's individual success.

In interviews, Jimmy is not always enthusiastic about the sessions he played, or some really remote groups he wrote for, or some records which feature the credit: 'James Page Music'.

He was featured on an album titled *Painter Man* by a group called Creation, which included violin bowing techniques which he adapted later in his career. He was keen on the theramin, an instrument much used by a group who called themselves Lothar and the Hand People, and which is evident in a different form on *Whole Lotta Love*, on Led Zeppelin's second album.

Perhaps one of the most informative features covering Jimmy's session work was printed in a three-part interview in the American magazine, *Trouser Press* — issues September, October and November, 1977.

THE YARDBIRDS

The decision to quit session work was made by Jimmy when brass sections and mass string arrangements became the norm, leaving less scope for experimental guitar work.

In June 1966, Paul Samwell Smith, bassist with the Yardbirds, decided to leave the group, and Jimmy agreed to fill in for him. He agreed initially to honor a few outstanding gigs, but later joined The Yardbirds permanently. Chris Dreja later took over the bass guitar role, leaving Jimmy to add a new dimension to the group's sound when he played dual lead guitar with Jeff Beck.

He had been a friend of Jeff Beck's since school-days, and their love of the guitar had encouraged them both to make or buy their own instruments.

Jimmy bought his first guitar — a 1949 Les Paul — on hire purchase for £200, for which his father acted as guarantor.

His work with The Yardbirds took him to America, Europe and many other countries, on tours which included college and club dates. The Yardbirds even did commercials for companies such as Coca Cola and Yardleys.

They were featured in the MGM film, *Blow Up*, where they were shown playing in a replica of the Ricky Tick Club. Their numbers included *Stroll On*, during the performance of which an 'agitated' Jeff Beck is shown smashing his guitar.

MGM issued a sound-

Circa 1967. The Yardbirds' last line-up. Chris Dreja, Jim McCarthy, Keith Relf and Jimmy Page (front).

Opposite Page: *The Yardbirds.*
This Page: Top: *Summer 1968. Jimmy onstage with The Yardbirds, USA.*
Bottom: *"Yardbirds onstage at The Shrine Auditorium, Los Angeles" to make live recording of "Yardbirds Last Rave-Up in L.A." Available only on bootleg and recorded over two nights on May 31 and June 1, 1968.*

track album for the film, but *Stroll On* was the only Yardbirds song to be featured.

In September 1966 the group undertook a tour of England with The Rolling Stones, Ike and Tina Turner, and Peter Jay and the New Jaywalkers (who featured a singer — Terry Reid — who particularly impressed Jimmy).

The group returned to America, after which Jeff Beck left the band and was not replaced.

They continued to record as a four-piece. Their first English releases did not receive the same enthusiastic response as they had received in America, where their album, *Little Games* (EPIC BN26313),

which had the same title as their first single, was released from the new line-up.

They had three hit records in America: *Little Games, Ten Little Indians* and *Ha Ha Said the Clown*.

Their last single with this line-up was *Goodnight Sweet Josephine*, which was withdrawn and is now valued as a collector's item (at around $300 for a mint copy at current prices).

A projected live concert LP, originally titled *Live at Anderson Theatre*, was also withdrawn, due to the group's disappointment with the quality of sound balance and the effect of overdubbing the sounds of cheering crowds.

The last phase of their career featured the group dressed in kaftans; these days they used psychedelic sounds, and by now

Jimmy was adopting the violin bow technique on stage for *I'm Confused*.

After touring to the Far East and other places, the band returned to England to perform a series of college and university gigs. They had appeared in a BBC Radio *Top Gear* programme, but by now the group members had grown restless, and decided to go their own ways. Their last gig as a group was at Luton Technical College in July, 1966.

The Yardbirds were one of the first groups to play experimental pop/rock music.

THE NEW YARDBIRDS

Although originally keen to stick with Jimmy and form a New Yardbirds, Chris Dreja later changed his mind and

chose to follow a career in commercial photography and design.

This left Jimmy with the group name, as well as several dates to fulfil in Scandinavia.

Together with Peter Grant, who had been with them in the last stages of the old Yardbirds, he formed the company Super Hype Recording, which freed them from recording under Mickie Most's production.

On hearing that Jimmy wanted to form a new group (from his wife, Mo, who had originally seen the advert), John Paul Jones contacted him.

Jimmy first traveled to see Robert Plant who had been recommended to him by Terry Reid, and later reported back to John that he liked what he had found.

Jimmy had considered session man B.J. Wilson

Top Left: *Chris Dreja, Jimmy Page, Jim McCarthy and Keith Relf.*
Top Right: *Jimmy Page with the Yardbirds in "Kaftan" era onstage in France.*

Club ads ('68-'71) courtesy the Howard Mylett collection; also the below early publicity pic.

Early Club ads.

for the drummer of the new group, but Robert told Jimmy of his friend, drummer John Bonham, whom he really wanted included in the line-up. After Jimmy had seen John Bonham in action with Tim Rose's backing group, he agreed, although when the offer was made to John it took him a while to decide to forgo the security of his former job.

The name New Yardbirds was retained, initially, because promoters seemed unwilling to book the group under another name.

John Paul Jones recalled the first time the group met: "It was in this little room — just to see if we could even stand each other! It was wall-to-wall amplifiers, and terrible. All old. Robert had heard I

was a session man and he was wondering who or what was going to turn up — some old bloke with a pipe! So Jimmy said, 'Well, we're all here — what are we going to play?', and I said, 'I don't know what, do you know?', and Jimmy said,

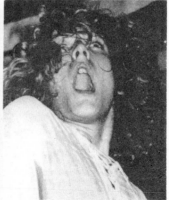

'Do you know a number called *The Train Kept a Rollin'*?' I told him 'No', and he said, 'It's easy, just G to A'. He counted it out and the room just exploded, and we said, 'Right, we're on, this is it, this is going to work!' And we just sort of built it up

from there."

John Paul Jones' career had been in session work. He was one of the youngest session men to be signed up as a musical director by Mickie Most. His first two records were, *Everything I Touch Turns to Tears*, by Barry St John, and *Land of 1000 Dances*, by the Cherokees. He took charge of Herman's Hermits' film music, and as well as being adept at piano, organ and bass, was much in demand by top British names of the 1960s, including Lulu, Dave Berry, Shirley Bassey, Kathy Kirby, Paul and Barry Ryan, Cat Stevens and Cliff Richard. Jimmy Page had also played sessions with many of these stars; the two players worked on Donovan's *Sunshine Superman* album together.

John's father was a pianist and arranger, who worked with big bands, and John's mother was a singer and dancer.

He was taught the basics of the piano, but became more interested in

Top Left: *Early 1969. Vintage Led Zeppelin group shot onstage at The Whiskey A-Go-Go, Los Angeles.*
Top Right: *Jimmy with psychedelic, painted guitar.*
Bottom Set: *Early Jimmy Page (top left) and Robert Plant onstage action shots.*

1969 USA tour. **Top Left:** *Jimmy;* **Top Right:** *John Paul;* **Bottom Left:** *Robert;* **Bottom Right:** *John Bonham.*

the organ.

His interest in bass guitar was due to his fascination in bass work generally. He used to turn up the volume of the bass on his record player and listen to the bass runs.

After gaining confidence on the instrument, he bought a Dallas Tuxedo bass guitar and home made amplifier, and joined a few local semi-pro groups.

He toured with Jet Harris and Tony Meehan, and played on their records. He also worked with the Rolling Stones on their *Satanic Majesties* album, and on string arrangements with them and other artists.

Robert Plant also had a varied career. Destined to become a chartered accountant with six 0-level passes at school in Stourbridge, Worcestershire, his involvement with music grew serious in his mid-teens when he joined a local, modern jazz club. He recalls: "It was quite a nice little scene with poetry and jazz. Lots of never going home, running away, sleeping bags and guitars. I was an apprentice beatnik."

He worked with a number of small bands in Birmingham, with groups such as The Band of Joy, Tennessee Teens, Crawling King Snakes, Black Snake Moan, and Delta Blues Band, playing country blues influenced by such artists as Memphis Minnie, Bukka

June 29, 1969. Royal Albert Hall Pop Proms action shots.

White and Skip James.

The Band of Joy was: "A sort of cradle for everything I really enjoyed in music. We used to specialise in the early Moby Grape stuff, the first album, and Buffalo Springfield and a few Love numbers.

"I liked Buddy Guy very much, things like *First Time I Met the Blues*, and that rough sound that came after Muddy Waters and Willie Dixon, really was devastating.

"I really admired Elvis Presley, because he was the first white guy to stand up there and really kick-it-out, really let loose."

Both he and Jimmy share an enthusiasm for the early 50s records produced on the American label, Sun. Robert says: "The energy that was put out in those early rock days was fantastic. Sam Phillips and Sun, and Ral Donner and Chuck Simmons; and it isn't nostalgia, it is sheer quality!"

EARLY SOLO RELEASES

With the exception of John Bonham the members of Led Zeppelin had released solo singles in their early careers. Although collectors' items nowadays, fetching over $100 in some cases, these have never reached the national charts.

In 1964 John Paul Jones had a single released on Pye (7N 15637), *Foggy Day in Vietnam / Baja*. This was his only single.

Jimmy Page released a solo in 1965. Titled, *She*

Just Satisfies / Keep Moving, this was virtually a one man band single, on which he played all instruments except drums (which were played by Bobbie Graham). The B side was an instrumental, with Jimmy on harmonica; the A side featured vocals by Jimmy; but *She Just Satisfies* was to be his only single (FONTANA, TF533).

In 1967 Robert Plant originally intended to record a song titled *Incense*, by the Anglos; however, on arrival in London at CBS to make his solo record, he found that the record company had a vastly different, preconceived idea of how he should be projected. So, the results of his solo efforts, at the age of eighteen, were: *Our Song / Laughing, Crying, Laughing* (CBS 202656), and *Long Time Coming / I've got a Secret* (CBS 202858).

Also in existence are some albums which feature Jimmy with other members of Led Zeppelin. These include *Three Week Hero*, which features all four members backing up P.J. Proby (1969, LIBERTY, LBL83219E), and *A Way of Life* by Family Dogg, which features all members except Robert (1969, BELL RECORDS, SBLL 122).

Robert cut a blues track entitled *Operator*, which appeared on a double anthology album by Alexis Korner (*Bootleg Hymn*, SRAK SP51), on the RAK label.

An album featuring Jimmy Page and John Bonham was Screaming

June 29, 1969. Royal Albert Hall Pop Proms action shots.

This Page: *Circa 1969. At-home pictures of Zeppelin.* **Top Left:** *Jimmy at his Pangbourne, Berkshire home;* **Bottom Left:** *Space-hopping John Paul;* **Top Right:** *Robert at the first farmhouse he bought and renovated for $16,000;* **Bottom Right:** *John Bonham plays a scaled-down version of his early kit.*
Opposite Page: *1971. Prior to the Vigorelli Stadium riot in Milan.*

Lord Sutch's *Lord Sutch and Heavy Friends* (ATLANTIC, 2400 008), issued in 1970. On the album Jimmy and John were made to appear as though they were playing alongside Sutch, but in fact they merely recorded several rock standards which Sutch later re-arranged. Sutch added his own lyrics and vocals, to the annoyance of Jimmy, for his and John's names were emblazoned on the sleeve.

John Bonham did not record any solo singles, but during his career prior to Led Zeppelin he played in a series of groups including The Way of Life, Steve Brett and the Mavericks, Terry and the Spiders and, at different times, he played with Robert in Birmingham-based bands Crawling King Snakes, and Band of Joy. At one stage he and Robert were blacklisted in their home area — in John's case because of the volume and power of his drumming, and in Robert's because of the volume of his vocals.

The combination of four idiosyncratically unique musicians who could draw on a wide and varied pool of influence, was a potent formula for the first Led Zeppelin recording. They worked towards a 'together' sound, amalgamating a fresh blend of blues and rock-with-basic- 'animal'-sounds, to Robert's soulful, powerful vocals.

The music was to be raw and basic, allowing for individual experimentation, and the first album forms a statement of the group's first two weeks together.

FIRST ZEPPELIN TOURS

Robert recalls being in the recording studio with the band for the first time:

Top: *1970. Onstage at Madison Square Gardens. Robert Plant, John Paul Jones and Jimmy Page.*
Bottom: *1969. Jimmy and Robert onstage at Paris Olympia.*

"It was such a big deal to have your voice come back through the speakers. I mean, I remember when we cut our first album and I heard *How Many More Times* come back through the speakers — I had one of the finest orgasms of my life!"

In America, on the strength of Jimmy's reputation with the Yardbirds as well as a recommendation from singer Dusty Springfield, the group were signed by Atlantic Records in a deal worth an alleged $200,000.

With the album completed by late 1968 at London's Olympic Studios, the group toured Scandinavia, and in October played a series of gigs in London, which included their first date as New Yardbirds at The Marquee (on October 16th) and their debut as Led Zeppelin at Surrey University later that month.

Manager Peter Grant followed up their first taste of onstage success with an American tour which took in the small cities. It was thought by some crazy not to head straight for the big arenas, but Peter knew the best way to build a sound market for the group. His experience of touring with English bands (notably The Animals) was a great asset to Zeppelin during their initial conquest of America.

On this first tour they played a prestigious concert at The Boston Tea Party. John Paul later recalled to journalist Steve Rosen: "We played for four hours, and we only had an hour and a half act, and so if anyone knew more than four bars of any tune we would go into it. We did old Beatles numbers and Chuck Berry numbers. It was the greatest night. We knew that we had definitely done it by then."

Robert praised Atlantic: "They did a good job with the white label copies of the first album, getting them out to the FM stations a couple of days before we got to town. We weren't even billed the majority of the time. But the reception we got was something else again, and that was especially surprising because in some of those towns the album had not yet reached the stores. After about the third number we could feel that the buzz coming back to us from the audience was different from the buzz the other bands got.

"When we played the Fillmore West in San Francisco, Bonzo and I looked at each other during the set and thought, 'Christ, we've got something!' That was the first time we realized that Led Zeppelin might mean something."

It was during this tour that the group began to stretch their numbers from their recorded form, and John Bonham formed a friendship with Carmine Appice of Vanilla Fudge. Carmine helped John get a

Top: *An early cartoon depicting Led Zeppelin.*
Bottom: *1972. Robert and Jimmy onstage in Australia. Jimmy has just got rid of his beard.*

sponsorship for his drum-kit with Ludwig.

Returning to England the group encountered a different type of audience. Their album had not been released yet, and although they drew considerable crowds wherever (including clubs and pubs) they played, it took word-of-mouth recommendations from fans who attended the gigs to consolidate their reputation.

America was a land more geared to youth music, so they decided to make America their main target. In America there was more chance of airplay, and more places for them to gig where their type of music would be appreciated.

FIRST ZEPPELIN ALBUM

Led Zeppelin's first album, entitled simply *Led Zeppelin* (ATLANTIC K40031) was issued in January in America, but not until March in England.

The album, with a cover design visualized by John Entwistle and the late Keith Moon of The Who (originators also of the name 'Led Zeppelin'), featured nine tracks:

Side One   *Good Times, Bad Times*
Babe I'm Gonna Leave You
You Shook Me
Dazed and Confused

Side Two   *Your Time is Gonna Come*
Black Mountain Side
Communication Breakdown
I Can't Quit You Babe
How Many More Times

Good Times, Bad Times opens with John Paul on classical organ sound heralding bluesy vocals and soaring guitar sounds. The group gels with a fine mixture of blues and heavy rock.

Babe I'm Gonna Leave You was the group's working of a traditional folk song and, at one point, an effect which sounds remarkably like an air raid siren, backs up Robert's angry vocals.

You Shook Me and *I Can't Quit You Babe* were the group's soulful musical workouts of two of Willie Dixon's original blues numbers, with plenty of bass guitar and intricate lead guitar work. Controlled drumming

Top: *Early '69. Newcastle City Hall, UK.*
Bottom: *Collectors' poster cards advertising early Zeppelin gigs.*

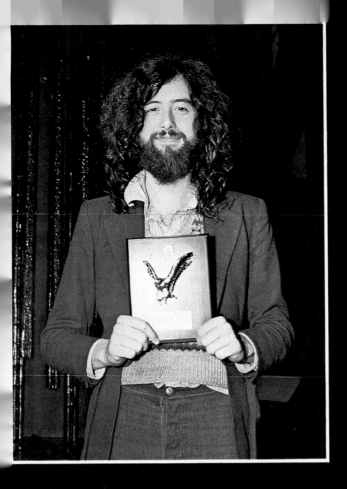
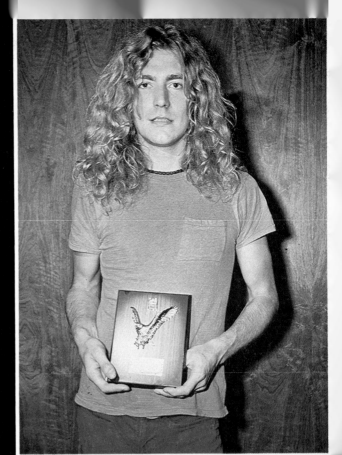
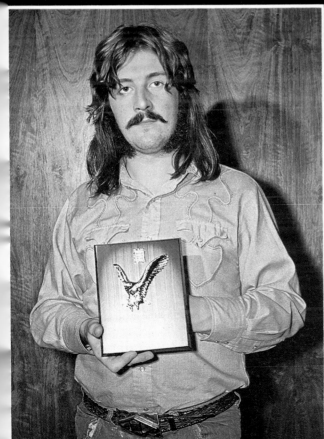

compliments Robert's effective vocals.

Communication Breakdown and *How Many More Times* seemed destined to become on-stage favourites as the group reach loud peaks of sound behind Robert's dramatic vocals.

Your Time is Gonna Come is an emotional song about a man spurned in love who seeks revenge. The feeling is captured powerfully by all group members.

Black Mountain Side features Jimmy on atmospheric guitar joined by guest instrumentalist Viram Jasani on tabla drums.

Dazed and Confused has doomy bass sounds opening the old Yard-birds' track, with Robert crooning and Jimmy play-ing mantra type violin bow guitar in the middle section. John Bonham's drums and John Paul's bass guitar re-enter the musical theme to round off the track in fine form.

In America, the record entered the album charts at number 98, and in a period of around six months reached the Top 5.

The record was a series of blues, folksy sounds and hard rock combined to make the record a very good musical debut album, lauded by some English critics and slagged mercilessly by some American critics.

For some, Robert's vocals were not too

pleasing, but others found his 'white blues-soul' lyrics to have depth and range of feeling, and noted that he worked part-icularly well with the three musicians in the group.

Jimmy, the 'known-to-the-public' member of the group, was sought out for interviews but made the point that he regarded John Paul, John Bonham and Robert musicians of equal importance to himself.

FIRST MAJOR ZEPPELIN VENUES

After the first album Robert concentrated his attention on developing the range of his voice.

Around this period the group were filmed for *Supershow*, the film which featured them playing *Dazed and Confused*, but unfort-unately at the time of film-ing Robert developed laryngitis, which some-what limited his perform-ance.

After the initial success of the album in America, the group toured there again in April for a fee four times that of their previous tour. This time they undertook the major venues, including The Fillmore and Winterland, where their concerts sold out.

Their act at these gigs was opened by their first-rehearsed song, *Train Kept a Rollin'*. Most of the material from the album was used and was well received. Robert's vocals empathized well with many of these numbers,

Top: *January 24, 1970. Leeds University.*
Bottom: *Circa 1968. Jimmy Page.*
Opposite Page: *Circa 1969. Vintage Jimmy. Shirne Auditorium, USA.*

1969. Gold albums for Led Zeppelin One album. Back: Peter Grant, Ahmet Ertegun (of Atlantic Records). Front: Jimmy, John Paul, John Bonham and Robert.

with he and Jimmy seeming to trade note-for-note, guitar and voice.

John Paul Jones, though musically powerful, seemed happy to stand a little behind the rest of the group. John Bonham, a very solid, hard hitting drummer played tastefully loud, with conviction and authority, against Jimmy and Robert.

Seeing them play live was becoming an experience. They had developed a sound which greatly improved on their studio work, and they played with such soul that some Americans were led to compare their style of music with the Chicago Blues of the 40s.

The group seemed genuinely bemused about their American success, but still strived to

improve on every performance. They helped turn on people to the blues, and they made music the way they had always wanted.

The inclusion of Jimmy's old Yardbirds guitar solo *White Summer* was often cause for a standing ovation. The crowd were riveted to the spot by the contrast between the sheer melody of the tune and the heavier numbers that had gone before it; they were bowled again by the encores, when the band ran through medleys of Chuck Berry, Jerry Lee Lewis and Elvis Presley rock'n'roll numbers.

Back in Britain in June, the group appeared on three BBC Radio concerts — The David Symonds Show on June 16th, Top Gear on June 23rd (both of

which allowed time only for a handful of numbers), and a one-hour Special from the Playhouse Theatre on June 27th.

They managed to include a blues number they particularly liked — Robert Johnson's *Travelling Riverside Blues*, which unfortunately was never released on any of their albums.

The following day, June 28th, they appeared at the Bath Festival of Blues and Progressive Music, attended by several thousand fans of the 'Underground' music world. They received little press, but were considered one of the most enjoyable groups on the bill.

The next evening, June 29th, they scored a massive personal triumph at the first night of The Pop Proms at London's

Royal Albert Hall.

Nick Logan, in *New Musical Express*, wrote: "The Zeppelin truly deserved the acclaim — it is boggling that in a matter of months they have achieved such a high degree of musicianship and become one of the biggest crowd pullers around. Concentrated touring has given them an extra edge in every department, and with drummer John Bonham and bassist John Paul Jones laying a solid rearguard, the frontal dialogue between Plant and Page has developed to a startling and stimulating extent.

"When the houselights turned off at 11 p.m. after one encore, the group returned to the stage to play *Long Tall Sally*, with the saxists from Liverpool

November 1971. Three shots from the "Electric Magic" concert at London's Empire Pool, Wembley.

Top: *Robert in action at London's Royal Albert Hall.*
Bottom: *1969. Awards ceremonial for sales of Led Zeppelin II.*

Scene and Blodwyn Pig, with the audience on their feet and dancing and a ticker tape reception of hand bills and balloons and petals of the flowers from the foot of the stage."

In July, Zeppelin returned to America for a coast-to-coast tour with Jethro Tull. At one New York venue 21,000 people turned up at an auditorium which could hold only 10,000. The promoter managed to squeeze in another 1,000 people but had to turn away the remaining crowds. The band were unable to accept the offer of $30,000 to appear again two nights later, having committed themselves elsewhere.

They received a gold record for a million dollars worth of sales for their first album. Already there were advance orders for 350,000 copies of their next album.

RECOGNITION AT HOME

The group were already working on ideas for their second album. They recorded, rehearsed and wrote in hotels, whilst traveling in London, Vancouver and New York.

In London, on October 12th, they played a Sunday concert at The Lyceum for reportedly the highest fee paid to a British group for a single concert.

26

During the concert, to a capacity crowd, Robert introduced some of their new numbers, and one journalist compared the reaction they received to "....the rebirth of the Fillmores."

Later the same month they returned to America, where they played at the famed Carnegie Hall, where the reaction was now typical: frenzy. A 30-minute drum solo by John Bonham was awarded a five minute ovation.

In December, their album *Led Zeppelin 2* (ATLANTIC K40037) was released, again with nine tracks:

Side One *Whole Lotta Love*
What is and What Should Never Be
The Lemon Song
Thank You

Side Two *Heartbreaker*
Livin' Lovin' Maid (She's Just a Woman)
Ramble On
Moby Dick
Bring it on Home

The album contained a variety of new ideas — *Moby Dick* with John Bonham's drum solo, Robert's Tolkien-influenced lyrics on *Ramble On*, the bluesy *Bring it on Home*, the inventive *Whole Lotta Love* with the mid-section channel-changing effect on guitar and theramin, and hard rock tracks like *Heartbreaker* and *Livin' Lovin' Maid*, which segue well together. *What is and What Should Never Be* is a building (from organ introduction) song with plenty of gutsy singing from Robert. *Thank You* is of a similar structure, with all

four group members to the fore. *The Lemon Song* is a good natured blues track with some fine guitar work complimenting the lyrics.

Throughout the album John Bonham and John Paul Jones add power and depth to the group's style.

On December 11th they were presented with two Platinum Records and one Gold by Mrs Gwyneth Dunwoody, Parliamentary Secretary to the Board of Trade at London's Savoy Hotel, for sales to America of five million dollars worth of records.

The new album topped charts in America, England and Europe. American Atlantic issued a shortened version of *Whole Lotta Love* from the album, which reached the top of the singles charts.

The group decided not to issue any singles in England as they felt that any singles would be "out of context", and were against the idea of "milking singles from within an album."

THE BEATLES CONQUERED

1970 opened with a short English tour set up by Peter Grant and Chrysalis. It had a title — *In Person, Led Zeppelin* — and the dates were as follows:

Birmingham Town Hall	January 7
Bristol Colston Hall	January 8
London Royal Albert Hall	January 9
Portsmouth Guild Hall	January 13
Newcastle City Hall	January 15
Sheffield City Hall	January 16
Leeds Town Hall	January 24

1970. Two shots from the Bath Festival, UK.

John Paul was now playing Hammond organ onstage as well as bass, revealing that Led Zeppelin had a quieter side. The group were performing with no support band, their sets still lasting well over two hours.

By February the group were off on tour again. A date in Singapore was cancelled because of objections to the length of the group's hair. Taking advantage of this they interrupted their travels and visited Bombay, where they also recorded. They then continued to Australia, and on February 21st, in Copenhagen, they played under the name of The Nobs because Countess Eva Von Zeppelin objected to the band using her family name.

After playing the Montreux Jazz Festival, the group traveled to America, where they played for one month to more capacity crowds.

They spent some time considering a possible full-length documentary film of their act but shelved the idea and turned down all offers to appear as guests on top TV shows, feeling that the sound quality of TV as well as the short exposure time it could afford them would not do justice to either their onstage act or their studio performance. Jimmy did make one guest appearance though, on BBC's Julie Felix Show, to play the acoustic *Black Mountain Side*.

In June, Zeppelin

November 1971. "Electric Magic" at London's Empire Pool, Wembley.

played a series of concerts in Iceland, then again returned to America where they turned down two dates at Boston and Yale to allow an appearance at the 1970 Bath Festival in England on June 28th. Cancelling out these dates meant a loss of $200,000 dollars, but they wanted to show themselves again to the British public.

Robert admitted to being uncertain of the reception they would receive at Bath, but after a few numbers the group roared through a driving set, which included an acoustic segment, and at the end of their performance they were called back for a total of five encores. For these they were forced to revert to their earlier rock'n'roll standards, to the audience's delight.

The next month, the now bearded group played a tour of Germany, breaking records for audience attendance at every stop along the way.

New material was being introduced into the set by the time they undertook their next American tour, in August.

In America, by now, they had become as big an attraction as the Beatles had in their heyday. In fact it was the Beatles whom they toppled from the National Pop Polls in September, in the British and International sections. Each Zeppelin member also either topped his respective category or was in the leading instrumentalist category in Melody Maker's results.

National press interest

Bottom: *1973 USA tour. Led Zeppelin beside their private Boeing 720B 'Starship One' jet plane.*
Top Left: *1973 USA tour. In action performing "Stairway to Heaven".*
Top Right: *1973 USA tour. The "Dazed and Confused" violin-bow segment.*

was aroused, and when presented with their awards (called 'Heavy Rocks'), they became front-page names.

Led Zeppelin Two came top of the British album charts in Disc magazine later that year. The group were pictured with Sandy Denny, of Fotheringay, who topped the Melody Maker polls as Best British Female Singer. Sandy joined Robert on a number projected for a later album.

History repeated itself on October 16th when Led Zeppelin, minus John Bonham, collected Gold Records for overseas sales to Europe of their second album, and Gold singles for more than a million copies to America of their single *Whole Lotta Love*.

After presenting the records, Mr Anthony Grant, Parliamentary Secretary to Trade, said: "The Government

recognizes the value of pop groups. Like other exporters, Led Zeppelin are in business, and if they're a success they deserve a pat on the back."

THIRD ALBUM, AND FIRST JAPANESE TOUR

When the group arrived back from their spring American tour earlier in the year they retreated to a small cottage named Bron-Y-Aur, in Snowdonia. The derelict building and the surrounding environment of the Welsh mountains lent itself to a productive spell of experimenting, rehearsing and recording, and provided the inspiration for their next album.

They entered the recording studios at Headley Grange in May, and the outcome was a ten track album (ATLANTIC DE LUXE 2401 002), some

tracks of which show the band's new direction. The album was released in October to a somewhat mixed reception:

Side One *Immigrant Song*
     Friends
     Celebration Day
     Since I've Been Loving You
     Out on the Tiles

Side Two *Gallows Pole*
     Tangerine
     That's the Way
     Bron-Y-Aur Stomp
     Hats off to (Roy) Harper

It's interesting to note that the finished tapes were mixed in Memphis, Tennessee.

Musical changes were evident in the folksy, pastoral feel of the two tracks *That's the Way* and *Tangerine*, and to some extent also in *Friends*, although the latter does build to a more 'electric' feel.

Since I've Been Loving You, with a mournful vocal and sympathetic guitar, illustrates the way Robert had worked on his vocal range — low key at

times, then a return to his soaring vocals showcased on Zeppelin's first two albums.

Gallows Pole contains some fine drumwork and tortured vocals set against the old Leadbelly blues number; guitars, banjo and mandolin are effectively introduced throughout by the combined talents of Jimmy and John Paul.

Hats off to (Roy) Harper was recorded as a genuine tribute.

Bron-Y-Aur Stomp showed Robert's influence, with the addition of John Paul Jones on five string fretless bass; the acoustic guitar, and Robert's on-stage dedication of the lyrics to Strider, conjuring up the image of a 'hoe-down'.

A Viking invasion is the subject of *Immigrant Song*, which has an opening war cry from Robert.

Both *Celebration Day* and *Out on the Tiles*

feature John Bonham in fiery form, evoking an impression of spontaneity and immediacy.

The album sat firmly at the top of the charts around the world while the group toured the Far East and appeared for the first time in Japan, where they were received almost as enthusiastically as they had been in America. They were the first of the new 70s rock bands to tread Japan's shores, and were given massive press coverage. The proceeds from one of their concerts was dedicated to the victims of the 1945 Hiroshima atom bomb, for which the Mayor of Hiroshima presented the group with letters of appreciation.

RIOTS - AND THE RELEASE OF A FOURTH ALBUM

After recording for several weeks, Zeppelin undertook the unexpected step of organizing a tour of the clubs — possibly to test audience reaction to new material. Ticket prices were fixed as low as possible.

But there was a sad lesson to be learned from this well-intended move, because for each person fortunate enough to find his way into the audience, another was unable to gain admittance.

The group spent March and April touring to as many small capacity venues as they could —

Top: *1969.*
Bottom: *November 1971. "Electric Magic" action from Robert.*

from London's Marquee Club, to Dublin. They featured their new number, *Stairway to Heaven*, which had Jimmy on double-neck guitar — a Gibson 12-string and six-string hybrid. In Dublin they were joined onstage for an encore by Phil Carson from Atlantic Records.

As the year progressed they continued to work on their fourth album, slowing down on the touring that had been so demanding the previous year; but whilst touring Europe in July the group was involved in the worst riot of its career. A crowd of 15,000 fans in Milan's Vigorelli Stadium were attacked by police and soldiers with batons and tear gas early in the group's set. The harsh action had apparently been caused by some fans jumping to their feet and clapping their hands. The band attempted to continue playing but the atmosphere became so thick with tear gas that they were forced to retreat to their dressing room.

They toured America again, to even larger crowds, and it was now only possible to place the 12,000-seater-plus venues.

Unfortunately, they found themselves playing less in England, though they set up an English tour for November, to take in the largest English concert halls and two nights at London's Empire Pool, Wembley.

These concerts, organized by Peter Grant and Rikki Farr of Buffalo Music, were titled *Electric*

Magic, and adventurously featured circus animals and side attractions, as well as supporting groups of their own choice (such as Bronco, and Home, from the Midlands, and Stone the Crows, with female vocalist Maggie Bell). The audiences for the two Wembley shows each numbered 9,000.

The tour coincided with the release of the group's fourth album. The album sleeve had no name; neither did the sleeve name the band. It was referred to in the album charts by four symbols, one for each member of the group. At first, it was believed that the symbols were Icelandic runes, but in later articles they were referred to as artistic symbols chosen by the band. [The symbols appear on the back jacket of this book, matched to their appropriate Zeppelin members — Publisher's Note.]

The album, which came with a printed word sheet for the track *Stairway to Heaven*, contained eight tracks:

Side One *Black Dog*
          Rock and Roll
          The Battle of Evermore
          Stairway to Heaven

Side Two *Misty Mountain Hop*
          Four Sticks
          Going to California
          When the Levee Breaks

The first track to catch attention, due to the inclusion of printed lyrics, was *Stairway to Heaven*. The song is a beautiful ballad with a slow, well paced acoustic opening. It progresses through some crystal clear passages, on

both electric guitars and drums, punctuated with bass, to a climactic build up and finish.

A drum introduction kicks off *Black Dog*, a fiery riff-trading rocker that includes some nice precision playing from Jimmy, John Paul and John Bonham. Robert provides out-and-out rocker vocals; a track that seems ever expanding.

Rock and Roll lives up to its title, and demonstrates once more the band's ability to work tightly as a unit. The number conjures up pictures of the band onstage — Jimmy stooped over his guitar imitating Chuck Berry's 'duck walk' across the stage. Repeated vocals add to the intensity of his screaming voice.

On *The Battle of Evermore*, the track which features the late Sandy Denny, both she and Robert seem to be racing to keep up with each other's vocals. Each compliments the other in a magical, Scottish folk song tinged with tales of the Dark Ages, while the guitars seemingly float in the background.

Misty Mountain Hop is a fast-paced number about a walk through a park and the Hippies encountered there. Some nice organ and guitar combinations throughout.

Four Sticks is a showcase for John Bonham. He plays as the title suggests. After some synthesized

Top: *1971 photo session.*
Bottom: *1972. Robert and Jimmy onstage USA performing "Dazed and Confused"*
Opposite Page: *May 5, 1973. Jimmy onstage at Tampa Stadium before a crowd of 56,800.*

1972. Robert and John Paul performing on tour, USA.

sounds from John Paul, Robert and Jimmy enter towards the end of the song (with John Paul on bass) to round off the tune. Robert's voice sounds inhumanly instrument-like.

Going to California is a romantic song sung to a delicate, intricate guitar accompaniment, about a girl 'with flowers in her hair'.

In sharp contrast, *When the Levee Breaks* is the group's adaptation of a Memphis Minnie blues track from the 1920s, with skull crushing drumming, slide guitar and hypnotic, trance-inducing vocals and guitars.

The album is a mixture of shifting moods, with imaginative music and controlled wildness.

WORLDWIDE TOURS

The group returned to live performances in February and March when, after playing New Zealand, they undertook their second tour of Australia. In Sydney and Auckland they played to outdoor crowds in excess of 25,000, and while in Australia, WEA managing director Paul Turner presented the group with four Gold records.

During the same year, an album, *The New Age of Atlantic* (ATLANTIC 20024), was released which included a Zeppelin track not featured on the group's own albums. With an

acoustic, bar-room sound, it was entitled *Hey, Hey What Can I Do*, and featured Robert singing about his 'woman who won't be true'.

When the group played their American tour during June and July they were still drawing capacity crowds, but press coverage of the tour seemed minimal compared with that given to The Rolling Stones, who were touring at the same time. The Stones were featured in both the concert reviews and in the social pages of the national dailies.

Zeppelin continued with their tour regardless, but they were keen to

convey their progress to English fans back home. The spirit within the band was at its peak, and their next move was to hire colorful media consultant man B.P. Fallon, who, like Peter Grant and Richard Cole, would travel with them on their dates, arranging interviews and ensuring that public awareness was brought to the group and its music.

The band made a short return to Japan later that year, and in November played two small hall concerts in Montreux for Swiss promoter Claude Knobbs. Fans from all over Europe clamored to get tickets.

An English tour was set

up to open at Newcastle City Hall on November 30th, and two days before Christmas the band played London's Alexandra Palace for two consecutive nights, before a total of 12,000 fans. They had had a high regard for the Palace, and thought that it would have made the ideal venue, but Robert afterwards claimed that it was a disappointment due to the coldness and the unsatisfactory acoustics for Led Zeppelin's music.

The tour featured previews of the forthcoming fifth album, and in Southampton they played a 'thank you' concert at the university venue 'Black Hole of Calcutta', or Old Ref as it is sometimes known. The standing crowd joined in the true spirit of the event, and were rewarded with a performance of *How Many More Times*, which was played for the first time in over two years.

After *Since I've Been Loving You*, the band performed two new numbers, *Dancing Days* and *The Song remains the Same*.

A mobile recording studio accompanied the tour, but the concert at the Old Ref, blessed with good acoustics, was the only concert to be recorded.

NEW MUSICAL DEPARTURES

At the end of March the group finally released the album they had originally hoped to tie-in with their previous English tour.

Titled *Houses of the Holy* (ATLANTIC K50014), the cover depicted a collage of blonde female infants ascending multi-tinted rocks. The design was the result of a combined effort between the group and designers Po and Storme of Hipgnosis who were responsible for some of the most impressive album covers of the period, for artists such as Pink Floyd, Syd Barrett, and 10cc.

Once again, the album had no obvious identification. A wrap-a-round strip of paper, printed with the lettering that was ultimately to become Zeppelin's own, was the only outward clue.

Eight tracks were featured:

Side One   *The Song Remains the Same*
            The Rain Song
            Over the Hills and Far Away
            The Crunge

Side Two   *Dancing Days*
            D'Yer Maker
            No Quarter
            The Ocean

The track *D'Yer Maker*, with its play on words of the phrase 'Did you make her?', and its good reggae feel, was released as a single in America, where the 'joke' lyric title was not familiar.

Another musical departure is *The Crunge* (doubling as the B side of the American single), which is essentially a James Brown pastiche, with Robert and Jimmy giving some good impressions on vocals and guitar backing.

No Quarter gives the album an eerie, foreboding feel. At times Robert's voice sounds as though it has been wired through some kind of filter. Onstage, this track was to become John Paul's musical interlude, sandwiched between a range of music from jazz to r'n'b to classical pieces.

The Ocean, which includes back up vocals from the whole band, has an infectious, toe-tapping feel, and is dedicated to the group's followers.

The Rain Song and *The Song Remains the Same* are both multi-layered, finely-structured tracks. *Rain Song* includes a strong mellotron section which sounds remarkably orchestral. John Bonham enters to emphasize the beat and crash-in on his Paiste gong. Jimmy's 12-string guitar fills out the at times almost pastoral feel, while Robert acts out the lyrics with full conviction.

The Song Remains the Same is Jimmy's tour-de-force, fully illustrating the capabilities and range of his double-neck guitar. It seems multi-tracked, and relentlessly increases in tension throughout.

Over the Hills and Far Away starts as an almost acoustic track, with extra instrumentation building throughout. Much of the latter helps punctuate the lyrics, which tell of 'dreams that have silver linings'.

Dancing Days is perhaps one of the hardest tracks to define, strongly reminiscent of 50s' Doo-Wop songs and summer evenings spent suppin' booze.

Houses of the Holy came with printed lyrics, and was a number one album in many countries including European countries. The band toured during March and April throughout Sweden, Germany and France, where the duration of the stage shows began to increase.

1972. Jimmy in high-kicking action shot on USA tour.

status of visual spectacle. The crew from Showco traveled ahead of the group to make the detailed arrangements that were necessary at each venue. From the opening tour in Atlanta Stadium in front of 40,000 people, they added a tremendous clarity to the act in the larger halls Zeppelin were now filling.

Zeppelin's mode of travel had changed also. Now they had their own private, converted Boeing 720B Starship One jet plane, which had been transformed from its original 138-seat plane into a 40-seat luxury liner containing bedrooms, bathrooms, showers, marble fireplaces, club rooms, bar, video machines as well as an electric organ. The group's name was emblazoned on the side of the plane in gold and bronze.

Speaking of Zeppelin's influences, Robert told American journalist Lisa Robinson: "We're into so many different things from Yehudi Menuhin to James Brown to Kaleidoscope. People don't just listen to Led Zeppelin or Snooks Eaglin, they listen to a number of things, and so do we. Our influences come from everywhere."

The tour was divided to allow the group to return home for a short break. After the break, on May 5th, they played Tampa Stadium to a record crowd of 56,800, and grossed $309,000, earning them-

'SHOWCO' SPECTACLE AND RECORD BREAKING CROWDS

The most adventurous tour of their career was their next in America, covering 33 cities, for which the group recruited the excellent special effects team, Showco Productions, of Texas.

Showco were responsible for highlighting Zeppelin's musical highspots with dry ice, mirror balls, back projected mirror, as well as superb lighting which included overhead spotlights and strategically placed overhead lighting. Adorned with these effects the concerts achieved the

Top Left and **Top Right:** *May 1975. Action shots from the series of five London Earls Court concerts.*
Bottom Left: *Circa 1975. John Bonham onstage, USA.*
Bottom Right: *1975, USA. Jimmy in one of many specially tailored stage suits.*

selves an entry in the Guiness Book of Records for largest concert attendance and largest gross in American history (previously held by the Beatles at Shea Stadium in 1965).

The group felt that the time was now ripe for a Zeppelin film, and hired a film crew to capture the excitement of three concerts held in July at New York's Madison Square Gardens.

After receiving Gold records for *Houses of the Holy* from Ahmet Ertegun at a party after the concert, the group headed back to England. While resting from the strenuous pace, individual Zeppelin members spent time working out personal 'fantasy' sequences for possible inclusion in their film. They were keen to see a finished product, and were aided at different times by directors Joe Massot and Peter Clifton.

John Bonham was filmed at Santa Pod raceway at the wheel of Clive Skilton's AA Fueler.

Robert was filmed riding on horseback in the beautiful Welsh countryside dressed in what could be described as 'historic costume'.

Jimmy played guitar on two tracks of the Maggie Bell *Suicide Sal* LP, while John Paul helped write and produce songs with Madeleine Bell for her LP *Comin' Atcha*, and was featured playing alongside

Top: *November 30 — January 30, 1973. Two shots of Jimmy performing on winter UK tour.*
Bottom: *1972 USA tour. Acoustic set with Robert and Jimmy. Jimmy has a strange axe.*

her on a BBC TV prog-
ramme based on most of
the material.

In the winter, Jimmy
traveled to his Scottish
home, Boleskin, which
was once the home of
Aleister Crowley, the man
described as 'the most evil
man in the world', but in
whom Jimmy developed
an avid interest. His
interest in Crowley
stemmed from his school-
days, and he felt that the
magician was in fact 'the
most misunderstood man
in the world', who had the
reputation of being the
one Edwardian able
positively to embrace the
20th Century.

In this setting, Jimmy
worked on his sequence

for the film, using the
effect of the moon
merging overhead into the
clouds...

THE SWAN SONG LABEL

The group spent part of
January and February in
the recording studio
rehearsing and working
on their 6th album. The
album was their first
double, and it drew from
a stockpile of tracks which
the band had wanted to
use on earlier albums but
couldn't due to lack of
space. An estimated half
of the tracks were drawn
from this source.

On February 14th,

Jimmy, Robert and John
Bonham joined Ronnie
Lane, the late Keith Moon
and Max Middleton on-
stage at Roy Harper's
Valentine Concert.

The Zeppelin, with
manager Peter Grant,
Pink Floyd and Charisma,
took their venture into the
world of filming one stage
further by financing the
film *Monty Python and the
Holy Grail* — a highly
successful comedy and
one of the few original TV
comedies to benefit from
the large-screen version.

Peter Grant and Ahmet
Ertegun put the wheels in
motion to form Led
Zeppelin's own record
label, Swan Song. The
label's design was inspired

by the painting *Evening,
Fall of Day*, by William
Rimner, and was to launch
their double album.

Of their reasons Robert
said: "The people involved
with us who will be on the
label — Maggie Bell, The
Pretty Things, Bad
Company (except Paul
Rodgers who was big
before with Free) were all
with record companies
that didn't do very much
for them. We're going to
try and pull it off for them,
and that's what this record
company means to me."

The group had parties
in New York and Los
Angeles to celebrate the

*November 1972. Onstage at Montreux for
Swiss promoter Claude Nobbs.*

Houses of the Holy, which they said had grown too complex.

Encouragingly for the label, the first Swan Song release — *Bad Company* — reached Number One in America's album charts.

The group's other signing was female singer Mirabai, whom they discovered on the New York club circuit.

There were no Zeppelin appearances during the year, though in August John Paul Jones played alongside Dave Gilmour, Steve Broughton and Roy Harper at an open-air Hyde Park concert in London.

Jimmy returned to America to jam onstage with Bad Company at Austin and Central Park's Schaefer Festival, joining them on both occasions after their first encore on *Rock me Baby*, to the American fans' delight.

Jimmy repeated this jam, this time with John Paul at London's Rainbow

formation of Swan Song. On hand were the artists signed, including Roy Harper, whose records would be issued on the label in America. Atlantic Records and Zeppelin employees were present, together with members of the press. In Hollywood the group's guests included the late Groucho Marx, Bill Wyman, Bryan Ferry and Micky Dolenz.

The group revealed that they had recorded many of the tracks for their forthcoming double — some tracks had been written before Christmas and some during their American tour. They added that they were returning to straight-forward hard rock, something they seemed to have lost on their last two albums, especially on

This Page: *November 1972. Jimmy performing at Montreux.*
Opposite Page: *1975. USA. Robert onstage.*

Theatre in December, when Bad Company had returned in triumph with Gold and Platinum records.

Swan Song was launched in England at a lavish, Zeppelin-style 'bash' in Chiselhurst Caves on Hallowe'en Night to celebrate the release of The Pretty Things' *Silk Torpedo*. In the candle-lit atmosphere of mulled wine, food, films reflected on the cave walls and disguised 'nuns' and 'monks', most of the Swan Song label artists were in evidence, as well as celebrities of radio and TV, including near-neighbor of John Paul, Adam Faith.

RELEASE OF PHYSICAL GRAFFITI

In January, Zeppelin played two warm-up dates at Rotterdam and Brussels, where Robert was interviewed by Bob Harris for TV's *Old Grey Whistle Test*. Robert hinted that the band were working on a special event in early summer for the English fans. He said that he thought the proposed Zeppelin film would be ready soon, and that Jimmy had been working on the sound track.

They returned to America for a tour which started on January 18th and went through to March 27th, but after Jimmy damaged a finger in a train door they were

November 1972. Robert onstage at Montreux.

forced to drop *Dazed and Confused* from their act — which was a shame because this was a five million dollar tour with no expense spared.

Laser beams and other startling effects were added to the already spectacular stage show.

During the mid-tour break their new double album, *Physical Graffiti*, was released on Swan Song (SWAN SONG SSK 89400/A & SSK 89400/B).

The album had one of the most imaginative and costly covers ever produced, and with fifteen tracks of varying musical shades and moods, it repeated the chart-topping success of its predecessors:

Side One	*Custard Pie*
	The Rover
	In My Time of Dying
Side Two	*Houses of the Holy*
	Trampled Underfoot
	Kashmir
Side Three	*In the Light*
	Bron-Y-Aur
	Down by the Seaside
	Ten Years Gone
Side Four	*Night Flight*
	The Wanton Song
	Boogie with Stu
	Black Country Woman
	Sick Again

Even the critics considered *Physical Graffiti* worthy of the wait. They admired a product that had come from such total, group dedication, and they were curious to know Zeppelin's new direction.

Custard Pie, with slurred, powerful vocals, synthesized moog and manic, hypnotic drums and guitar riffs, has all the force of Zeppelin in full flight.

The Rover is a reflective, driving song recounting travels. It carries the lovely line, 'If we could just join hands', which it repeats to good effect over some fine chord structures.

In My Time of Dying is Zeppelin's restyled version of a Bob Dylan number. It has one of the hardest hitting, dramatic vocals, backed with powerful drumming and an ominous, almost obsessive chant, 'Got to be my Jesus-oh, take me home'.

Houses of the Holy pioneers a 'new' guitar sound from Jimmy. Almost loose lyrics, referring to Satan's daughter, implore: 'Let the music be your master'. An effective overdubbed guitar enters at the end of the track.

Trampled Underfoot features John Paul on clavinet, and has insistent, nicely synchronized drums and guitars. Robert says that the song is about: "...the motor car, although it has nothing to do with cars—just moving parts." Onstage this track was visually especially pleasing, with Robert emphasising the closing 'Push, push' phrase.

Kashmir. Spellbinding, symphonic, majestic, neo-classical, mesmerising, ethnic — just a few of the adjectives that have been used to describe this building, epic track which conjures up so many pictures in the mind...

In the Light is another

November 1972. Robert at Montreux.

example of Zeppelin's diversity. The droning introduction sounds almost like the cry of a whale. Robert's vocals are double tracked, at times tender, always changing to fit the mood set by the music.

Bron-Y-Aur is an abrupt change of pace; a warm, lilting, beautiful acoustic solo from Jimmy.

Down by the Seaside features some unusual, laid-back vocals, with John Paul on electric piano; another lighter side of Led Zeppelin.

Ten Years Gone falls into the Zeppelin 'type' of stage-improved studio composition. Robert sings of first love, the love never forgotten, and features Jimmy's overdubbed guitars.

Night Flight is a return to the hard rock the group play so well. Robert emphasizes the lyrics with power, and John Bonham turns in a fine, tight drum sound.

The Wanton Song is apparently the type of number the Band of Joy once played. Dramatic, sweeping vocals and guitar riffing.

Boogie with Stu is another un(a)typical Zeppelin song. Ian Stewart, who worked

Top Left and Bottom: *1972. Action shots from the UK winter tour.*
Bottom: *1972. Action shot of Robert onstage, USA.*

with the Rolling Stones, plays some nice piano, which suits the slapping, good-time feel of the track, and adds a 'live' quality.

Black Country Woman has some reflective, bluesy vocals from Robert. John Bonham adds some fine drum-kicking passages against Jimmy's and John Paul's lighter guitars.

Sick Again features some frantic guitar work. The rock 'feel' bumps and grinds, relating encounters on the group's American travels.

"Every album that we've done has been different, and that's not a conscious thing but more a natural evolution," Jimmy Page said after this album was released.

As an added sales incentive Swan Song released a limited edition single (of 5,000), *Trampled Underfoot / Black Country Woman*, which was issued to the trade at the rate of one copy for every 20 Zeppelin records ordered.

By the time Zeppelin reached the Madison Square Garden's date, Robert was shaking off a cough together with the remains of 'flu, though John Bonham was suffering from stomach problems he attributed to nerves. But Jimmy's finger had improved — enough to warrant the re-introduction of *Dazed and Confused*.

The number showed spectacular imagination. During the violin-bow section green and purple lights and smoke surrounded Jimmy with a demonic 'triangle'. Green lasers beamed out over the heads of the audience. Other effects included a series of explosions which occurred at the rear of the stage. Giant lights,

December 1972. Onstage at the Brighton Dome, UK. Note Jimmy on back up vocals in lower shot.

positioned above the stage, spelled out the group's name.

The tracks from the new album, which by the end of the tour were becoming crowd favorites, were greeted with roars of approval.

John Bonham's health improved, and on one occasion he bought a $1,400 Ford Hot Rod for the purpose of 'dragging' on Sunset Strip. In two weeks dragging, during which he raced with any-one who would accept his challenges, he was stopped only once. Bad Company's Mick Ralphs was his passenger, and John told the speed cop that he and Mick were musicians who'd been rehearsing and were letting off steam. He escaped without a ticket.

The tour regenerated interest in the recorded works of the group, and all six of their albums were featured in Billboard's Top 200 Album Charts.

EARLS COURT

In May, Mel Bush and Peter Grant presented the group's first English concerts for two years at London's 17,000 seater Earls Court. Because of overwhelming ticket demand the concerts, which had originally been planned to number three,

Top: *1972/73 UK tour. Jimmy abandons plectrum for violin bow.*
Bottom: *May 5, 1973. Historic concert at Tampa, Florida. Zeppelin broke attendance records before an outdoor audience of 56,800.*

were extended to five. The national press picked up on the band's American tour, and The Sun, the Daily Mail and the Observer Color Supplement carried extensive features.

The original tour dates were May 23rd, 24th and 25th; the two additional dates were May 17th and 18th. Each concert lasted around three to four hours. Ticket prices were from £1 to £2.50, for which fans were treated to the extra effects from the group's American tour. A video screen was positioned to the right of the stage to give those in the back of the arena continuous close-up images of the band.

After the announcement 'Welcome Home,

Led Zeppelin', the first concert opened with *Rock and Roll*.

Two of the songs performed, *In my Time of Dying* and *Kashmir*, were dedicated to the then taxman, Chancellor of the Exchequer Dennis Healey, and to the English city of Bradford, respectively.

Kaleidoscopic lights were directed from the side of the stage during an improvized performance of *Trampled Underfoot*, which featured pounding drums, blistering guitar and frenzied vocals.

The acoustic set contained four-part harmonies. *Moby Dick* featured phased tympani drumming as well as a hand-drumming style: the £4,000 video screen showed John Bonham's

body movements and facial contortions synchronized perfectly with his grunts and mutterings as he built towards a violent, explosive and impressive climax, hitting the gong with his bare hands.

The closing number was *Stairway to Heaven*. The audience demanded two encores. Finally Robert, dressed in an open-chested top and denims, rounded off the evening with the announcement "Goodnight everybody, it's been a great night".

After the concerts Chris Welch of Melody Maker visited John at his Worcestershire home. He showed Chris around the farm, explaining his new interest as a stockbreeder. He also showed Chris a trio of powerful 'hot cars'. One of these, an elaborately painted vehicle mounted on three-foot-wide wheels which he had bought in Los Angeles, was capable of speeds of up to 150 mph. The other two cars were a 1967 Corvette with a 7-litre engine, and a 1954 two-door Ford with an 8-litre engine.

He recalled buying a white Rolls Royce, which he drove to a wedding reception in Birmingham. When he came out the Rolls had been jumped on, the windows smashed and the windscreen kicked-in.

Before the Earls Court concerts the group had rehearsed for three days, to 'remove the rust'. They

Top: *January, 1973. Jimmy onstage at Southampton University "Thank You" concert, UK.*
Bottom: *William Burroughs, author of the novels "Naked Lunch" and "Cities of the Red Night" and originator of the term 'Heavy Metal'. From the 1960s to the present day a whole succession of rock acts owe their names and some of their numbers to Burroughs' characters and ideas—Soft Machine, Steely Dan, Insect Trust, Dead Fingers Talk, David Bowie to name but a few.*

p.49
1977 USA tour. Jimmy onstage in dragon suit.

had spent a long time rehearsing for the American tour because they liked to change the show each year.

John told Chris: "We keep tapes of every show, and it's useful afterwards, especially for my drum solo because then I can hear what works best. Before the Earls Court concerts it was so cold in the arena that I was playing in an overcoat. I try to play something different every night for the solo but the basic plan is the same, from sticks to hands and then the tymps and then the final build up. There have been times when I've blundered and got the dreaded look from the lads, but that's a good

sign, it shows you're attempting something you've never tried before. Once we start into *Rock and Roll* I'm fine. I just can't stand sitting around, and I worry about playing badly, and if I do mess it up then I'm really pissed off. If I play well I feel great. Everybody in the band is the same, and we each have some little thing we do before we go on, like pace about, or light a cigarette. You might have to sit around for a whole day and you daren't have a drink because you'll get tired out and blow it. So you sit and drink tea with everybody around saying 'Far out, man'."

He told Chris that in Britain the group never

got airplay except from John Peel and Alan Freeman, whereas in America their records were played all day.

MELODY MAKER POP POLL AWARDS

After Earls Court the band organized some much needed individual holidays for themselves. When they had refreshed themselves they planned to tour round the world and then back to England, playing possibly in South America, Hawaii, Japan and Asia Minor, ending up with dates in Europe.

In July there were reports that Jimmy, Robert and John Paul

were now tax exiles living in Switzerland. But on August 4th, whilst still on holiday on the Greek island of Rhodes, Robert and his family were seriously injured when

their hired car crashed into a tree.

Two Harley Street doctors and blood plasma were immediately flown out to help the family, who were then air-lifted back to London.

Maureen had fractures of the pelvis and a suspected fractured skull, and was concussed for 36 hours. Robert had multiple fractures of his ankle and elbow, but their children, who were fortunately in the back of the vehicle, sustained only minor injuries.

The tax laws of the time prevented Robert from remaining with Maureen, who was confined to bed for several weeks, and he was therefore forced to stay in Jersey, spending a

Top: *1973. John Bonham onstage at Southampton University "Thank You" concert, UK.*
Bottom: *May 5, 1973. The massive crowd of 56,800 at Zeppelin's attendance-breaking Tampa Stadium concert.*

long spell on crutches while he recuperated.

He became restless, and after several weeks arranged to rehearse and travel with the rest of the band.

During a stint in Los Angeles the Melody Maker announced their Pop Poll winners, and Jimmy flew to London's Carlton Tower Hotel to receive on behalf of the band a grand total of seven Awards.

Billy Connolly, who presented the Awards, told his audience (which included John Bonham): "The next section is quite

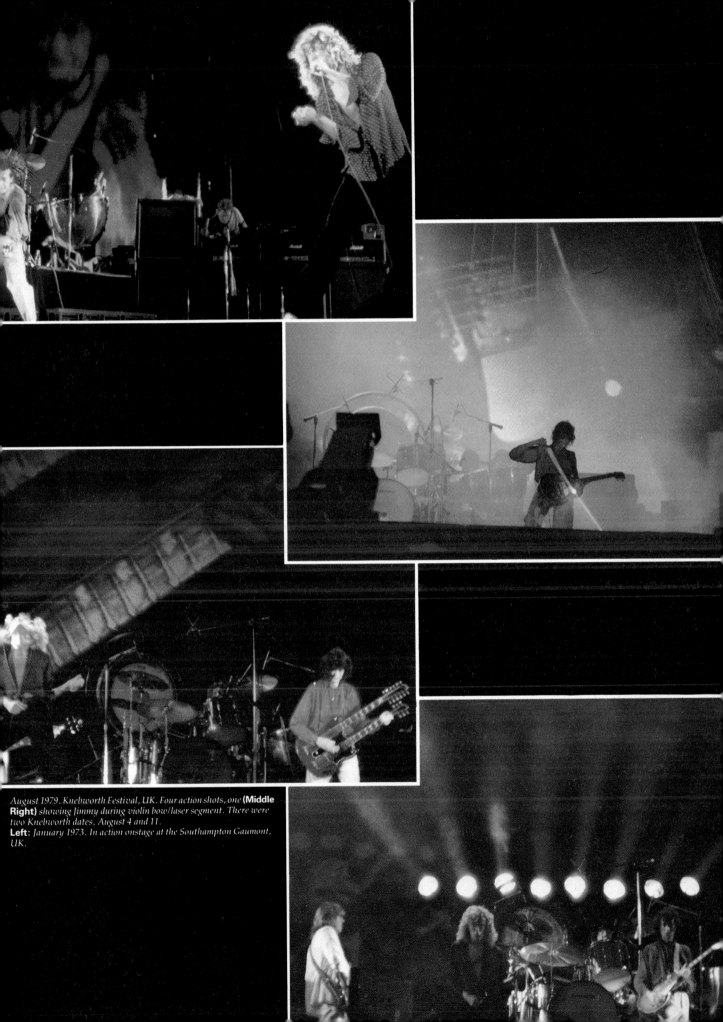

*August 1979. Knebworth Festival, UK. Four action shots, one (**Middle Right**) showing Jimmy during violin bow/laser segment. There were two Knebworth dates, August 4 and 11.*
Left: *January 1973. In action onstage at the Southampton Gaumont, UK.*

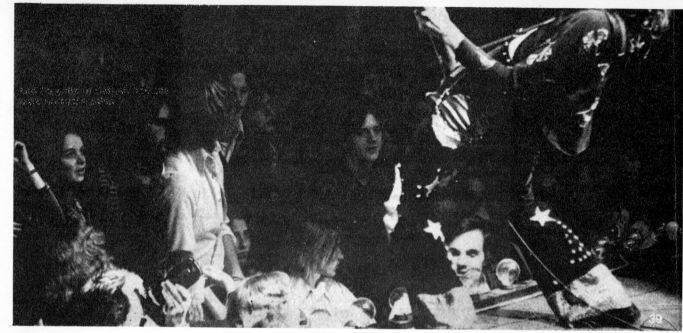

staggering!'' — and proceeded to reel off the list of prizes scooped by Led Zeppelin. Top Male Singer (International) was won by Robert; Top Album (International) was *Physical Graffiti*; Top Guitarist (International) was won by Jimmy; Top Male Singer (British) was won by Robert; Top Album (British) was *Physical Graffiti*; Top Band (International) was Led Zeppelin; and Best Live Act (International) was Led Zeppelin.

After the Poll, John Bonham, in an interview for TV, was asked whether the band had been surprised to receive so many awards. His modest reply was: ''The awards usually go to the group that happens to be touring at the time. That's when the kids can see you. Earls Court is the best thing we've done in this country.''

When asked if the awards were an inspiration, or whether they were regarded by the band as being 'something for the mantelpiece', he replied with an obliqueness that was typical of him: ''I still got nervous today sitting at the table listening to the awards being read out!'' Some bands, he said, had blasé attitudes towards awards, but this was not the case with Led Zeppelin. ''The real 'earthmovers' are as nervous when they're receiving awards as they are when they do a concert.''

Talking about the birth of his daughter Zoe, he said: ''We went 'non-resident' officially after the last tour. I lost days because I stayed home, as my wife was having a baby. There was no way, for any money in the world, I was going to go away. I wanted to stay at home, and I missed out as far as the last tour was concerned.''

After the writing and rehearsing period in Los Angeles and Malibu, the group moved on to Munich to record their

Top: *1975. Jimmy at front of stage in Detroit.*
Bottom: *September 1975. Jimmy, his daughter Scarlet and John Bonham at the Melody Maker Poll Awards presentation. Zeppelin collected seven awards.*

next album (the album which was to become Jimmy's personal favorite Zeppelin album).

For Robert the album related specifically to 'a moment in time', and a lot of it was a record of their hurt. There was a feeling of immediacy in the tracks, which were cut in only 18 days.

During the recording Robert, mainly seated, narrowly avoided re-opening his fractured foot when he tripped over in the studio.

It was actually work which kept the group from drifting apart during this period, but it was to be some while before the album could be released due to a delay in the preparation of the ambitious cover artwork. Before its release, Robert spoke with Lisa Robinson in New York:

"There is so much determination on the album, fist-banging on the table. It's full of energy because of that sort of primal fight within me to get back to work, to get better and whole again." Like John Bonham he was now finding as much fulfilment at home as playing with the band.

"Benji LeFevre, who was responsible for making me sound brilliant (laughs) onstage before, and now has helped me get through all this, went down to my farm and saw for himself what a great thing it is there. Maureen (Robert's Calcutta-born wife) is as pretty as ever, and we're both improving. I like to think that she's come out of it with as much freshness as I have."

Publicly it was a quiet period for Zeppelin, though the New Musical Express of February 21st 1976 showed a snap of the group playing at Behan's night spot in Jersey. Robert was seated, and they were 'sitting in' with the resident rock pianist Norman Hale for a 45-minute set, performing a mixture of rock songs before a crowd of 350.

RELEASE OF 'PRESENCE'

In April, after the delayed cover art was finished, the new album entitled *Presence* was released (SWAN SONG SSK 59402). The work of Hipgnosis, the album again bore minimal descriptive information, but was elaborately visual. It featured ten 'situation' shots — and a mystical Kubrick-like 'object'. The latter attracted a good deal of attention from fans and journalists bent on decipherment, but no one could get beyond the fact that, like Zeppelin's music, the object had 'presence'.

The object is at the center of each situation, bearing the same significance to contemporary life as Kubrick's object had

1975. Spectacle is added to stage presentation. USA.

The "Zeppelin Over Europe" tour. **Top Left:** *John Bonham;* **Top Right:** *John Paul;* **Bottom Left:** *Robert;* **Bottom Right:** *Jimmy.*

borne to the ages of Mankind in *2001: A Space Odyssey*.

The group's name and the album title were embossed on white at the top right-hand corner of the sleeve. There were seven tracks:

Side One *Achilles Last Stand*
For Your Life
Royal Orleans

Side Two *Nobody's Fault but Mine*
Candy Store Rock
Hots on for Nowhere
Tea for One

A track that seemed particularly relevant was *Tea for One*. According to Robert this song arose from the loss he felt separated from Maureen after his car accident. At first listen it strongly resembles the bluesy *Since I've Been Loving You* — well structured, and lots of feeling.

Nobody's Fault but Mine is based on a much slower version of a Blind Willie Johnson 1920s song. Robert is on harmonica. Jimmy and Robert (who places slurred, drawn out emphasis on the word 'nobody') make a return to their guitar-matched-to-voice arrangement, while John and John Paul add a relentless, attention-grabbing beat.

The influence of Elvis Presley's early songs shines through on *Candy Store Rock*, with some nice Sun — almost Rockabilly — tones. There's a rawness and depth to this that may be missed until listeners give it more than one or

58

two plays.

Achilles Last Stand is the track that caused Robert's near-accident in the recording studio. Both John and John Paul feature prominently on this very busy track. Jimmy builds up a virtual battery of guitars, the whole generating a feel redolent of Robert's 'fist-banging' — though in this case the feeling is optimistic, looking forward to a future of 'eternal summers'.

Robert returns to slurring vocals on the soulful *For Your Life*. The song contains a wealth of different guitar styles, ranging from tremolo note-bending, to rhythmic and controlled soloing,

with all instruments gelling well. Another facet of Zeppelin 'sound'.

Royal Orleans contains guitar sounds similar to those delivered in *The Crunge*. Robert relates 'goings on' in Orleans,

while John repeatedly uses hissing cymbals to add to the frenetic sounds.

Hots on for Nowhere has a bouncy, swing feel with contemplative lyrics which sing the wisdom of the proverb 'Look before you

leap'.

By the end of April *Presence* was topping the album charts worldwide.

In America, on May 23, Jimmy and Robert joined Bad Company onstage at their Los Angeles Forum concert for the encore which featured *I Just Wanna Make Love to You*.

Through their shared love of Rockabilly Robert came to talk with Dave Edmunds, who subsequently signed to Swan Song and produced several successful singles.

Robert also traveled to the Cardiff Rock Festival in June to watch The Pretty Things in action. John Paul had jammed with them on May 27th on piano, playing *Route 66*, at London's Marquee Club.

'THE SONG REMAINS THE SAME' — FILM AND ALBUM

October 1976 — the month many Led Zeppelin fans had been waiting for — saw the release of Zeppelin's film, *The Song Remains the Same*.

The national press was approving. Journalists noted the film's honesty and lack of pretentiousness, its typical Zeppelin qualities. 'The Most Faceless Faces since Howard Hughes', was how one journalist had once described Jimmy, Robert, John and John Paul. The film portrayed the group while remaining true to the band's intention to keep their music pure and uncolored by personalities.

Throughout America and England audiences

received Zeppelin on the big screen almost as enthusiastically as they had received them live at concerts.

Robert described the film as being a record of one gig at Madison Square Gardens, its scenes intercut with fantasy and sequences that captured the ambience of a Led Zeppelin concert. The film works on several levels, contrasting life on the road with life at home in England, showing the inner minds of Led Zeppelin, and above all standing as a powerful record of their music.

Peter Grant and Richard Coles take the roles of gangsters in the opening scenes, conveying metaphorically their attitude toward the manipulation of talent in the entertainment world.

A continuous build-up of speed and intensity enhance the group's appearance on stage. The musical power of Led Zeppelin in concert attacks the audience like a wall of sound. At strategic points during this assault the 'fantasy' sequences are inserted. Each sequence is personal to a member of the group.

In the first Robert, dressed in suitable garb, lands on a northern shore in a Viking-type craft, and in a castle scene that owes a lot to his interest in history, is shown fighting for the 'ultimate' damsel. His theme is the one of Life-as-a-journey, and his intention is to portray the incidents that occur along Life's path.

John Paul's part is a

Top: *1975 USA tour.*
Bottom: *1975 USA tour.*

mixture of his first love —
his music — and a bizarre
night rider dressed in a
grotesque mask. The film
returns to the tranquillity
of his family set-up, and
features his wife Mo and
children Keira, Tammy
and Cindy in period
costume.

John Bonham's
sequences, considered by
Jimmy to be the best
because they depict John's
true character, show John
in hot rods and on motor-
bikes, roaring down
country lanes at break-
neck speed, playing pool,
on the building sites,
enjoying a drink in the
local, showing off his live-
stock, and at home with
wife, Pat, and son, Jason.
Jason plays a scaled-down
version of John's drum
kit. The sequence contains
the action-packed scene at
Santa Pod Raceway at the
wheel of Clive Skelton's
AA Fueler, which drew
spontaneous applause
from many of the
audiences, especially the
Americans.

Jimmy's scene is power-
fully imaginative. Time is
the predominant theme,
showing him as he sees
himself from old age to
embryo and then in
reverse order. The scene
which contains his ascent
of a mountain, which he
had hoped would
incorporate a shot of a full
moon shining on snow
(an idea which was
spoiled due to the fact that
the cameras had not been
set up in time and the
snow had melted by the
time they were) is never-

theless breathtaking
because of his use of yoga
training and laboratory
work.

The film, financed by
the band, lasted for over
two hours, and had its
premiere at New York's
Cinema One Theater,
where $25,000 were raised
for the Save the Children
Foundation.

In England the film was
discussed on BBC's *Old
Grey Whistle Test* TV
programme, in which
Peter Grant and Robert,
on a boat on the Thames,
were shown being inter-
viewed by Michael
Appleton. They insisted
that television was not the
right market for the
group's music, and
declared that the TV rights
for the film were not available. In another interview
Peter told a reporter that
he had viewed film of the

Top: *1975 USA tour.*
Bottom: *1975. John Paul, official photo.*

End of 1980. Four shots from the "Zeppelin Over Europe" tour.
Top Right *and* **Bottom**: *The concert at Dortmund;* **Top Left**: *The concert at Cologne;* **Middle**: *John Bonham and Robert at the last-ever Zeppelin date in Berlin.*
Left: *1975. Robert and Jimmy onstage, USA.*

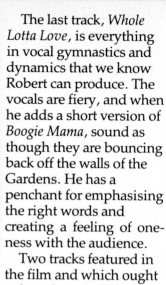

1975. John Bonham in "Clockwork Orange" boiler suit and bowler. Official photo.

Earls Court concerts through a standard TV screen, and came away with his feelings reinforced.

The film had originally been recorded in 4-track stereo for screening at select theaters, but public demand eventually caused it to be shown in standard theaters.

A double album of the film soundtrack was subsequently released (SWAN SONG SSK 98402). Carrying the same name as the film, it received praise from the press for being a *soundtrack* rather than a live album. The nine tracks are as follows:

Side One   *Rock and Roll*
             Celebration Day
             The Song Remains the Same
             Rain Song

Side Two   *Dazed and Confused*

Side Three   *No Quarter*
             Stairway to Heaven

Side Four   *Moby Dick*
             Whole Lotta Love

The opening notes of *Rock and Roll* kicks off the album — a high energy start which powers through the speakers of record player or cinema PA with equal effect.

The pace continues with *Celebration Day* (curiously not featured in its entirety in the film), and with the title track, which is more powerful than the original; the atmospheric vocals and a relentless instrumentation is made more atmospheric by the 'in concert' feel.

Dazed and Confused is what many Zeppelin fans wanted to hear — if they've ever enjoyed hearing the improvization the group used onstage. This 26-minute-plus version demonstrates just how brilliant a musician Jimmy is. The track features some of the most demonic sounding guitar / violin bow effects ever to appear on record. It contains as well a wide variety of other guitar sounds. The film illustrates the use of finger playing, while

Robert joins in and ad-libs with Scott McKenzie's *San Francisco* lyrics.

Stairway to Heaven is a 'song of hope', and these introductory words set the mood for the philosophical lyrics. Memory of the superb visual effects found in the film enhance this version.

The version of *Moby Dick* demonstrates how the track has progressed from its original to the excellent stereo separated intricate work on this outing.

The last track, *Whole Lotta Love*, is everything in vocal gymnastics and dynamics that we know Robert can produce. The vocals are fiery, and when he adds a short version of *Boogie Mama*, sound as though they are bouncing back off the walls of the Gardens. He has a penchant for emphasising the right words and creating a feeling of oneness with the audience.

Two tracks featured in the film and which ought to have been included on the record are *Autumn Lake* played by Jimmy on hurdy gurdy (when he is first introduced on screen), and *Since I've Been Loving You.*

MAMMOTH AMERICAN TOUR

In January 1977 the group rehearsed at Manticore Studios in London for their upcoming American tour. Originally scheduled to start in February the tour was later rescheduled to an April date, due to illness (Robert suffering from tonsillitis).

They spent some time checking out the 'new wave' groups in the clubs around London and in March, minus John Bonham, played a pub 'gig' at The Crocodile Pub in Dane Hill, warming up on old rock standards.

After opening on April 1 in Dallas, they played four nights at the Chicago Stadium, from April 6 to 10, although one of the dates was cut short after one hour when Jimmy

was taken ill on stage. He had reached the point where he was chain-smoking during the act, and was ordered to rest-up.

In Minneapolis the group landed on the runway in their newest version of personal transportation, a 727 jet, which bore on its fuselage the Swan Song logo together with the group's name.

Piling into a fleet of waiting limousines, the group and their sizeable retinue of roadies, technicians and tour administrators as well as American reporter Stephen Ford, traveled to the Minneapolis Sports Arena. A police escort of eight motorcyclists took them speeding through traffic and street intersections directly into the arena.

On arrival, in this typically Zeppelin 'military' fashion, a team of security men called out orders through walkie-talkie radios, and as the group reached the back stage garage area they were ushered into the dressing rooms.

The area behind the stage contained an array of pre-amps, monitors, laser-beam units, highly sophisticated consoles for mixing and balancing the audio, and a score of 'flashboxes' electronically triggered on cue — all operated by a small army of technicians.

On hand here, as always, is Peter Grant, the man as much responsible

for the group's success as the group itself. Peter acts as a guardian, hovering over his four charges amid reports about the mood of the audience, security measures and the arena's acoustics. As well, he conducts all financial dealings with the box office manager.

He is aware of the causes of disruptive elements in the audiences and considers the main cause of unruliness to be the festival seating arrangements which have no facility for reserve seating. At some venues the fire marshals state the allowed maximum audience capacity.

John Paul told Stephen Ford: "We all have very different personalities offstage, and I think that's why we've lasted so long. Robert and Jimmy dote on the recognition, and that's great for them. Bonzo and I prefer the anonymity. I like the idea of being able to go any-where without a lot of people carrying on. I'd rather Robert and Jimmy take the spotlight because someone in the band has got to be exciting, you know, capture the imagination of the public. I think if all four of us wanted the glory there'd be fights. We'd have broken up years ago. I can see most of our American audience now is under 21, but I don't feel silly performing for a 15-year-old crowd. We've been doing that for quite a few years and each new generation of 15-year-olds likes our music, so we must be doing something right.

Our secret is we're flexible, and we all like each other."

A practise the group employed to relieve the rigors of the road was to set up a permanent base of operations as often as they could. During their tour of America's Midwest, for instance, they stayed at Chicago's Ambassador East Hotel, flying out early each evening to wherever they were engaged, and returning to Chicago and their rooms after the concert.

"You'd be amazed at what a difference that makes," Robert said to Stephen Ford. "Instead of packing bags every day, doing the show, unpacking at a different hotel that night, then repeating it all the next day. When we do the East Coast we stay in New York and do the same thing."

At the Silverdrome when the lights went down for the start of the

three-hour-plus show, at around 8.20 pm the darkened building erupted with fireworks and rockets, and thousands of lighted matches burned in the darkness.

Some of the cherry bombs made monstrous 'booms', but when the group appeared, the stage erupted even more loudly. The drums and bass literally shook the building. The Silverdrome's acoustics, renowned for echo and reverberations, hardly intruded though; instead the sounds seemed almost to be a part of the show.

The enormity of the event, the extra-large video TV screens complete with replays, as well as the excitement built up over weeks of waiting, helped create an awesome atmosphere. The group were in top musical form.

Many critics recognized the group's strength of

popularity after two years absence from American concert halls, and after most of the once-great practitioners of the over-amplified 'art' of heavy metal (a term Led Zeppelin dislike when applied to themselves) had either toned down their approach or packed up their amplifiers Zeppelin maintained the strong aura of mystique built around them.

The volume necessary for the massive venues at times affected the group's hearing, and Robert told the crowd at one venue that he was deaf in one ear at the start of the concert but was relieved when his hearing came back during a later number.

In an interview with friend and American DJ, J.J. Jackson, John Paul told of a concert in Santa Monica when, because of deafness, he was unable to hear his bass playing during the entirety of the

1975. Onstage, USA.

show; but a fellow musician told him afterwards that his playing had been some of the best that he had heard.

On the tour, America's rock presenters and city and county ordinances enforced strong restrictions on cans, bottles, alcohol, audio and visual reproduction equipment, cameras and tape recorders and so forth. Para-medics from the Seattle Fire Department were on hand before the show.

Despite restrictions, the April 28 Cleveland concert was recorded unofficially and appeared as a four-album box set entitled *Destroyer*; another four-album set *For Badge Holders Only*, was produced from the Los Angeles Forum June 23 concert, and features Keith Moon guesting on drums for *Moby Dick*.

Mounted police sat on their horses in the middle of the crowds, and when an official wanted to stop the crowd from surging into the ticket gates, the mounted police would simply position their horses sideways, so blocking the entrances.

Aboard the group's private plane Robert wandered around with small groups of people, enjoying the food, champagne and pina coladas (a drink popular among the group), although John Bonham seemed content to mingle with the passengers while sipping on a quart of beer.

Jimmy seemed quiet on the plane, and ventured occasionally to the bar, and John Paul settled for a game of Backgammon.

Asked about rowdy crowds, Robert said, "We are used to them, but it can be crazy. A lot of times they break up our concentration. I'm watching Jimmy, or the group's watching me for a cue and suddenly a frisbee sails out of the audience and none of us sees it. We've all been hit by these on-stage, but the firecrackers are much worse. They scare the hell out of us."

The American press coverage of the tour was vast, and spawned several one-off Zeppelin magazines, including a publication titled *Led Zeppelin Versus Kiss*, and a superb concert program, *An Evening with Led Zeppelin*, a large format book-come-program featuring 42 color in-concert pictures, strangely without text.

The group drew a 76,229 crowd at The Pontiac Silverdrome, and police and stadium officials were amazed by the relative tranquillity of the massive throng of people. The gates had been opened two hours beforehand to avoid a build-up of impatience among the fans.

During a break in the tour, on May 12th at London's Grosvenor Hotel, the group were presented with the prestigious Ivor Novello Awards (called 'Igors'), for their contribution to British Music. The awards were presented by comedian John Inman.

Present were Robert, Jimmy, John Paul and Peter Grant. The Awards Programme contained a reproduction of the *Led Zeppelin One* album, as well as a 'Thank You', and the words 'Nice One Ivor'.

Melody Maker of June 25th carried a four-page article on the tour, its front page calculating that an estimated 1,338,729 fans would see the band on the tour (due to continue through until August 13th.)

Among their engagements was a return to Tampa, Florida, where they had made entertainment history, but this time, on June 3, at the open air stadium, it began raining 20 minutes into the set. Since the rain was sheeting into the stage mouth, threatening the band with electrocution, Zeppelin were reluctantly forced to call off the concert, and refunds had to be made to the 70,000 disappointed fans.

The original itinerary of the grand tour totalled 51 dates. Six of these were at Madison Square Gardens. Ray Coleman described these as being: "A crucial point in the tour. The group are touring against a background of that much daunted feeling of deja vu surrounding such 'dinosaur' bands — a whiff of an attitude that there are so many *new* bands coming up that, well, haven't we seen all this supergroup stuff before? To their evident delight — for the four

1975 USA tour.

musicians have been smiling a lot in this week in New York — Zeppelin have well and truly laid that bogey to rest.''

120,000 saw them at Madison Square Gardens, and during June 21 through to June 27, the same number saw them at the Los Angeles Forum.

With an average performance time of three hours, a set that featured normally fifteen numbers, with selections from most of their albums, and two encores which normally consisted of *Whole Lotta Love* and *Rock and Roll*, and a stage show that was, to say the least, theatrical, though not self-indulgent, the group each received acclaim for the way their act had developed. Perhaps the film had given just that bit more insight into the band, playing in this Jubilee Year (for Britain), with Robert toasting 'The Queen' and raising a cup of tea to several audiences on the tour.

John Bonham was surrounded by a battery of tom toms, an artillery of drums, and a gigantic gong, and during his solo, in which he and his kit were taken nearer to the crowd on a drum riser platform, he played a mammoth session made stronger and more visual by complimentary lights, dry ice and flames, to delighted audiences.

John Paul, amid lasers and dry ice, was a quiet tower of power on bass, and exceptional on keyboards. He looked a majestic figure during his delivery of *No Quarter*, with its mixture of musical departures. Later, during the group's acoustic set he introduced a new instrument, a triple-necked guitar, as well as a stand-up bass.

Robert was commanding on stage, his injuries from the car accident seeming to have left him un-impaired. The sheer power of his vocals rein-forced his role as 'the heart and lungs of the band'. Ray Coleman praised his voice, which he found 'in good shape with all its blazing ferocity, and haunting quality on *Stairway to Heaven* and *Ten Years Gone*'.

Jimmy was dressed in a white satin dragon suit and shades. Sometimes, later in the tour, he wore SS cap and baggy britches and knee-high boots. His tireless movements inclu-ded several acrobatic jumps, while lasers syn-chronized perfectly with the notes from his guitars, drawing roars from the crowd.

In his review of the tour Ray Coleman claimed that Jimmy must be the arms and legs of the band, to utilize such a wide range of original styles. His was the work of a 'demonic craftsman'.

But after playing two concerts at Oakland Stadium before 110,000 fans, tragic news reached Robert. His son, Karac, was seriously ill. The five-year-old was rushed to hospital with an enteritis-type infection, on Tues-day July 26, but was dead on arrival. A shocked Robert immediately went to his Blakeshall Estate to be with his wife, who was under sedation, and his daughter, nine-year-old Carmen Jane.

England's Daily Express of Thursday July 28th carried a front page head-line, 'Pop Millionaire Mourns His Son'. The accompanying article reported that Maureen had telephoned Robert in New Orleans, where the group was only ten days away from the end of their tour; the tour had been

postponed, and later cancelled, as Robert chartered a jet home to England. The article spoke volumes when it quoted Robert's father whose few words were: "All this success, what does it mean when you compare it with the love of a family?"

Knowing the close family bond, many thought this heralded the end of Led Zeppelin's career, and in fact a considerable time elapsed before more was heard of any member of the band, and speculation of their impending split became rife. Finally, in late October, Jimmy emerged to tell the press: "After the tragedy that Robert experienced he needs time to be alone with his family. Zeppelin's so close that no one person within the band would think twice about that situation. There is no question of splitting up. I know Robert wants to work again, and he'll start working again at his own pace."

In October Jimmy played a 45 minute impromptu set with Ron Wood and Arms and Legs for the Goaldigger's charity at his then local public house, Plumpton's "Full Moon".

In May 1978 the group were reported back in action, rehearsing inten-sively at Clearwell Castle in the Forest of Dean, for what was hoped would be a new album or tour. In June Robert started jamming with local bands, the first with the unusual name of Melvin Giganticus and the Turd Burglars, with whom he played rock standards in small clubs.

John Paul and John Bonham played a 'super-session' at London's Abbey Road with Paul McCartney and Wings. The guest list also included Pink Floyd's Dave Gilmour, Pete Townshend, and Hank Marvin. In October they were featured on two tracks, *So Glad to See you Here* and *Rockestra Theme*, on an album arising from

the session entitled *Back to the Egg* (EMI PCTC 257).

In November, Robert was active playing five-a-side football at London's Empire Pool, Wembley, following which the group returned to the London rehearsal studios for six weeks of work. Robert also took time out to jam with Midland-based band Little Acre.

As the year drew to a close Zeppelin visited Abba's recording studio, Polar, in Stockholm. They liked the atmosphere as well as the helpful attitude of Abba, and decided to settle in to start recording — up to January 1979.

KNEBWORTH

With the exception of John Paul, Led Zeppelin returned to Stockholm in February 1979 for the mixing of the new album. But before this Robert's wife, Maureen, gave birth to a son, christened Logan Romero.

BBC Radio's Friday Rock Show featured a repeat of the two June 1969 Radio Concerts, which reminded fans just how good the band had been early in their career.

In a period that was (for Zeppelin) fairly low-key, Robert was reported jamming with Worcestershire band Melvin's Marauders (in May), but otherwise spent as much time as he could with his family.

The best music news in 1979 for English fans was undoubtedly the confirmation later in May that Zeppelin would play Knebworth Festival on August 4th. In June a second date was added, for the following Saturday, August 11th, with Keith Richard's and Ron Wood's group, New Barbarians.

As a warm up for the dates Zeppelin played two gigs at Copenhagen's Falconer Theatre on July 23rd and 24th. At the first gig the generators supplying the stage sound and lighting effects developed problems, and because each gig attracted an aud-

Top: 1977, UK. John Inman (to right of photograph) presents John Paul, Peter Grant, Robert and Jimmy with Led Zeppelin's Ivor Novello Awards.
Bottom: *1977. The onstage power of Jimmy and Robert.*
Opposite Page: *May 1975. Onstage at London's Earls Court.*

ience of about 2,000, the band were none too pleased. Robert referred to the July 23rd concert as 'disastrous'.

The Knebworth Zeppelin dates were organized by Frederick Bannister, the Festival Organizer, in association with Peter Grant, and each were scheduled to run from 11 a.m. to 11 p.m. The line-up included Zeppelin-chosen acts, among whom were Todd Rundgren, Southside Johnny and the Asbury Jukes, Fairport Convention, Chas and Dave, and Commander Cody.

A week before the concert was due to start, fans camping on or near the site heard the group run through a sound check, during which John Bonham's 11-year-old son, Jason, took his father's role on *Trampled Underfoot*. The performance prompted John Paul to remark: "It was amazing to hear drumming in the same powerful style as John, and to

Top: *1977. USA. Acoustic set.*
Bottom: *1977 USA tour.*

see the smaller figure of Jason handling the number so capably."

Although an estimated crowd of 150-200,000 attended the two dates the events went smoothly, with police constantly on hand to direct the pedestrians and traffic arriving at the massive site.

During the long wait for Zeppelin's appearance on the first day, the crowds were entertained by the support groups, and by Nicky Horne, Capital Radio's DJ. The denimed multitudes, basking in the sun, had to suffer a further 20 minute delay while technicians perfected the excellent sound system. Finally, the opening notes of *The Song Remains the Same* rang out around 9.40 p.m., and the group

appeared, dwarfed by a huge video screen at the back of the stage which projected giant images of the group in action.

Despite the cold and dark of the evening, and the period of Zeppelin inactivity since the American Tour of 1977, the degree of fanaticism from the crowd seemed unequalled.

Here, as in Copenhagen, they featured two songs from their upcoming album, *In the Evening*, which was an instant crowd pleaser, and *Hot Dog*, with an up tempo Rockabilly sound.

The set lasted three-and-a-half hours, and featured approximately 20 numbers, and evoked three encores. This more than pleased their fans, although among music

Top: *1977 USA tour. "Jimmy Page's body catches the excitement; his mind bleeds through his guitar."*
Bottom: *1977, USA. An atmospheric pose.*

revolving pyramid of laser lights. The beams of light changed shape as Jimmy, waving a luminous red-tipped bow, climaxed in a spinning cone — nothing short of dramatic!

In the final song of the set, *Stairway to Heaven*, the audience lit matches, and, holding them aloft like miniature torches, joined Robert's vocals — a participatory event that added a tremendous personal feel to the 'anthem'. The group left the stage, returning to play three encores, taking the crowd well into the morning.

After the final encore, *Heartbreaker*, many left the site and promptly set up camp to repeat their date with Zeppelin on the following Saturday (which differed from the first in its exclusion of *Ten Years Gone*, and the *inclusion*, in the encore, of *Communication Breakdown*).

RELEASE OF 'IN THROUGH THE OUT DOOR'

Knebworth was a milestone for many, especially for the new generations of

world 'intellectuals' of the time it had become unfashionable to speak favorably of the group or of their performance.

By the time *Nobody's Fault but Mine* was performed the band had achieved an impressive tightness, with John Paul and John Bonham working closely together, and Robert and Jimmy sharing the spotlight with the scat parts of the lyrics.

Intensity was the keynote of *Since I've Been Loving You*, which paid tribute to the band's blues roots. This led into John Paul's solo in *No Quarter* which featured a reduced

version of the song while allowing the classical and blues passages to shine through.

The center of the stage was set for a seated version of Jimmy's *White Summer* solo. With the aid of flashpots, and with the stage bathed in the rays of a 'desert sunset', the solo led into a spellbinding version of *Kashmir*.

Achilles' Last Stand (the song Robert called 'The Wheelchair Song') was performed next, to excellent effects again from the best light show of the time.

The center section of *Dazed and Confused* followed, and featured Jimmy with violin bow and Gibson, coaxing out a series of wonderful sounds amid a giant,

Top: *1977 USA tour. John Paul with triple-neck guitar.*
Bottom: *July 1977. John Bonham dressed as druid behind Jimmy at Zeppelin's last-ever concert at Oakland Coliseum.*

fans who made a discovery in Led Zeppelin.

The crowds contained people from all over the world, each of whom will hold in their minds a favorite moment from the dates, yet Robert admitted afterwards that his voice suffered from nerves during the early part of the first set. The group themselves were in awe of the size of the crowd, and the confidence that the crowd had in the group.

After the trials and tribulations, Robert considered the concerts 'an act of communion with the English folk', and because the fans weren't sure what to expect from the band after their lay-off, he compared the encounter to a 'blind date.'

Both Jimmy and Robert had spoken of a proposed commemorative single they had hoped to have on sale at Knebworth. According to Robert this was to have been along the lines of the music of Clash and Sham 69, but due to a shortage of time, was never released.

The release on August 20th of the new Zeppelin album, *In Through the Out Door* (SWAN SONG SSK 59410), was simultaneous worldwide. Sleeve design was by Hipgnosis, in collaboration with Jimmy and Peter Grant. A buff outer sleeve bore the track titles and the group's name. Inside were two

July 1977. Jimmy and Robert take a few seconds' rest at the Oakland Coliseum concert.

areas of the drawing would produce color-ations.

By mid-September *In Through the Out Door* was Number One on both sides of the Atlantic, and stayed at Number One in America for a record seven weeks. Like its predecessor it reactivated interest in the catalogue of Zeppelin albums, all of which featured in Billboard's Top 200 Album Charts.

It also gave a boost to the flagging record industry in America during one of the industry's worst ever sales slumps.

The seven tracks were as follows:

Side One *In the Evening*
           South Bound Suarez
           Fool in the Rain
           Hot Dog

Side Two *Carouselambra*
           All my Love
           I'm Gonna Crawl

inner sleeves, the first depicting a bar scene in sepia, and the second a black-and-white drawing.

There were six different versions of the bar scene, the design showing the bar on each occasion from the viewpoint of differing persons within the scene. The innermost sleeve was 'impregnated' so that strategically dampened

South Bound Suarez opens with 'pumping' piano, and develops into an epic, driving number, similar in construction to *Custard Pie*. It contains some tasteful guitar work, and

Top: *1977 USA tour.*
Middle: *1977 USA tour. Victorious Jimmy holds guitar aloft onstage.*
Bottom: *1977 USA tour. Front stage view.*
Opposite Page: *1977 USA tour. Jimmy onstage in Ohio.*

Top: *1977. New York.*
Bottom: *1977 USA tour. Jimmy and Robert in the light.*

the theme of the song is echoed by Robert's repeated vocals.

Carouselambra is an extended piece utilizing a variety of tempo changes. John Paul takes the movement, with heavy emphasis on synthesized passages. Complex lyrics in a song of majestic sound and quality.

All my Love is a personalized, melodic song with a nice hook. Short, sweet and to the point, it has an effective mid-section 'trumpet' sound. A song which Robert called: 'A natural extension of *Stairway to Heaven*'. It proved to be the most requested track in America.

I'm Gonna Crawl, after a 'string'-sounding opening, develops into a Wilson Pickett / Otis Redding, slow rhythm'n'blues. According to Robert its lyrics are about 'the things you do for love or for a woman you need badly'.

Fool in the Rain is an unusual track for Zeppelin, said to be influenced by the carnival-type ambience of the 1978 World Cup in Argentina. A samba-like beat heralds an unusual drum sound from John Bonham, who adds great 'feel' to the track.

Hot Dog is a mixture of country rock and rockabilly, dedicated to the State of Texas and to the people of Texas.

In the Evening is the instantly memorable track with phased tympani drum opening which leads into a skilful blend of keyboards, synthesized strings and stinging guitar passages from Jimmy. Another track filled with 'majesty'.

In America the album was praised for its all-round qualities of performance and excellence in engineering. In

the latter field it was an album that went unrivalled in 1979.

More than any other this album showed the creative excellence of John Paul, and re-emphasized John Bonham's position as the musical backbone of Zeppelin. "I got to the studio with Robert before the others," was John Paul's modest response to this acclaim.

Fool in the Rain was taken off the album, for release instead as a single in America. It reached the Top Twenty Singles Chart. But the proposed follow-up, *All my Love*, the most requested track there, was not released.

After Robert's return visit to Wembley's Empire Pool for another five-a-side soccer match on November 25th, the Melody Maker Poll Awards for 1979 were published. Led Zeppelin were winners of seven categories: Best Live Act, Band of the Year, Best Album, Top Guitarist, Top Producer, Top Composer and Top Male Singer.

The awards took the form of mounted semi-

Bottom: *1977. John Bonham tips his hat to the crowd at Madison Square Gardens.*
Top: *1977 USA tour. Jimmy and John Paul.*

quavers, which were presented to the band at a reception at London's Waldorf Hotel by ex-Monty Python star, Michael Palin. Only Jimmy was absent.

On December 26th, listeners to BBC Radio London were treated to *Echoes*, a 90-minute program presented by Stuart Colman and featuring Jimmy and Robert in conversation, who played some of their all time favorite records. It was recorded in October, and held over as a Christmas attraction. The band revelled in the opportunity to retrace their musical roots and interests, but commented sadly on their discovery, on American tours, that artists whom they admired were still playing small clubs, sometimes for meagre fees.

The BBC had more in store, and broadcast, this time throughout its regions, a repeat of a 1969 Zeppelin radio session, 'In Concert'. To round off this

Top: *1977. Scarf and shades 'look' for Jimmy onstage.*
Bottom: *1977 USA tour. John Paul on stand-up bass behind Robert and a chain-smoking Jimmy.*

active week, on December 29th the band (minus Jimmy) played at the UNICEF Rock for Kampuchea concert at London's Hammersmith Odeon. They joined Wings' headlining evening, playing for one night only. Robert played alongside Dave Edmunds and Rockpile on the old Elvis Presley song, *Little Sister*, and later the three Zeppelin members were featured in the 'star spangled' Rockestra Section of the evening's encore when they played on *Lucille*, *Let it Be* and *Rockestra Theme*.

1977 USA tour.

'LED ZEPPELIN OVER EUROPE'

On January 16th K-Tel Records issued a compilation 13-track benefit album, *The Summit*, in aid of the Year of the Child campaign. It featured *Candy Store Rock* by Led Zeppelin, and contained a special 'Thank You' for Zeppelin for the band's help in its compilation.

America paid honor to the group when rock magazines Creem and Circus declared them Number One in virtually every nomination. *Stairway to Heaven* was claimed as being *the* Number One song of the 70s.

Robert made a guest appearance with Rockpile in Birmingham in February, and in early March John Bonham recorded a 'segment' for the Tyne Tees TV magazine program *Alright Now*, on which he was interviewed by Billy Connolly.

In late April, Zeppelin spent several days rehearsing at London's Rainbow Theatre. A press announcement to this effect, however, soon forced them to seek new premises, at London's New Victoria Theatre.

Top: *1977 USA tour. John Bonham. Official photo.*
Centre: *1977 USA tour. Classic action shot of Jimmy with Les Paul guitar.*

Then news came of a European tour, organized in conjunction with Harvey Goldsmith.

Originally scheduled to start in May, in Vienna, after revisions and further rehearsals at Shepperton Studios, a new date of June 17th, at a Dortmund venue, was fixed.

The other dates on the short tour (which was thought to be a prelude to an American tour) were Cologne, 18th; Brussels, 20th; Rotterdam, 21st; Bremen, 23rd; Vienna, 26th; Nurenburg, 27th; Zurich, 29th; Frankfurt, 30th; Manheim, July 2nd & 3rd; Munich, July 5th; Berlin, July 7th. The sets lasted approximately two or two-and-half hours, and pulled crowds of between four and ten thousand.

Onstage, Jimmy was dressed in a series of baggy suits or trousers, whilst Robert wore his usual green tee-shirt and jeans with hair cut approximately to its 1969 length. Ironically, the opening number of the tour was a song from the same era, *Train Kept a Rollin'*, from the Yard-birds days. On this occasion the song was

Top: *August 1979. Knebworth Festival, UK. A bank of guitars lie to the right of the stage; a giant video is located behind the group. Also in the picture are friends, families and management.*
Bottom: *1979, Knebworth UK. Onstage action.*

preluded with a blistering guitar introduction from Jimmy on wah-wah pedal, and set the mood for the shows.

The revitalized act contained fewer effects than previous tours, with the exception of flashpots, kaleidoscopic lights and a strategically placed light which shone brightly into the audience during the performance of *Trampled Underfoot*.

No Quarter was omitted from the acts, as were Jimmy's violin bow section and the lasers.

The set consisted of a basic 13 numbers, including *All my Love*, which was reproduced faithfully onstage for the first time.

At these moderately-sized venues, closer rapport was developed between group and audience. Jimmy in particular seemed more forthcoming than usual in this respect, endlessly crossing the stage, at times immersed in his playing, at others happy to venture close to the crowd. For the first time he introduced to the audience (on *Black Dog*), sometimes speaking to the crowds in their native tongues — a gesture not necessary for the strong

contingency of English and American fans who cropped up at many of the dates, following the group as often as they could.

Good humoredly, Robert asked the audiences to join him in a 'thinker' pose, and to repeat the phrase 'I Thank You' — a chant that soon became the tour catch phrase.

Top: *Jimmy in "Laser Cone pyramid" during guitar solo.*
Bottom: *1979. Knebworth.*

There was a noticeable absence of British press on the tour, though there was fairly extensive European coverage. A one-page article by Steve Gett covering the Munich concert was featured in Melody Maker. This was the concert at which Bad Company's Simon Kirke, using his own drum kit, joined John Bonham (for the encore, *Whole Lotta Love*), and which also featured the *Let That Boy*

Boogie segment. Some of the concerts featured old Elvis Presley numbers. The theramin was in evidence again, and Jimmy joined on back-up vocals for *Whole Lotta Love*.

Steve noticed that the group appeared to enjoy themselves as much as the audiences, and in conversation the band spoke of their renewed enthusiasm in their work as well as their wish to work again in England.

At Nurenburg the concert was halted after only three numbers when John Bonham was taken ill. On examination he was diagnosed as suffering from physical exhaustion, and arrangements were made for him to rest. He was considered fit enough to resume work in Zurich, but stomach trouble plagued him during the latter part of the tour.

Other highlights of the tour, on encores, included a spot in Frankfurt when Phil Carson joined in on bass on *Money*, and the performance of *Communication Breakdown* at Manheim.

In the heat of some of the summer evenings after only a couple of numbers the group were sweating profusely, and during some numbers whenever Jimmy shook his head sweat visibly poured from him.

At most of the concerts the standing crowds were often only a few feet away from the stage.

Two souvenirs of the tour are readily available — a Japanese book entitled *Viva Rock*, featuring color and black-and-white shots from several of the concerts,

Top: *July 1979. Onstage at the Falconer Theatre, Copenhagen. One of two concerts which were intended as 'warm-ups' for Knebworth.*
Bottom: *1979, Knebworth UK.*

and *Tight but Loose*, the Led Zeppelin magazine edited by Dave Lewis who traveled on the tour and who managed, comprehensively, to cover onstage and off-stage events. He reported some interesting conversations with Robert, who welcomed comments and who seemed to be in a particularly analytical mood when questioned about the group's performances.

It was felt that this tour was the one which would regenerate Robert's interest in touring. He

Top: *1979, Knebworth UK. Robert, John Paul and John Bonham. Official photo.*
Bottom: *August 1979. Knebworth. Maureen, Carmen Jane (in 1973 Zeppelin T-shirt) and Robert backstage for a family photo.*

asked Dave Lewis humorously, "Where's the British Press been so far? Maureen's beginning to wonder if we're doing this tour at all!"

John Paul's dry wit was in good form, and he confided that *No Quarter* had been dropped because it had become "a bit of a burden" to him.

Jimmy, in good spirits, confided: "I just want to play and play. I get off so much on the feed-back this group gets."

John Bonham, although dogged by stomach trouble, added: "Over all, everyone has been dead chuffed with the way this tour's gone. There were so many things that could have gone wrong. It was a bit of a gamble this one,

but it's worked really well.''

The magazine also featured interesting contributions from the group's personal roadies — Raymond Thomas (for Jimmy), Mick Hinton and Rex King (for John Bonham), Alan Leadbetter (for John Paul), and Benji LeFevre (for Robert) — as well as from Peter Grant and tour promoter Harvey Goldsmith.

Along for several of the dates was Richard Bunton and Chris Turner (four of Chris Turner's pictures appear in this book). They were fortunate enough to meet and talk over drinks with the group, who seemed accessible and friendly to fans.

Unfortunately, although this was the band's first tour since Knebworth, no souvenir programs were produced. Instead a color poster of the group was released from Swan Song on which appear photographs of the band taken shortly before the tour. Also released were badges and sweat shirts bearing the slogan 'Led Zeppelin Over Europe '80' together with the image of a skyward-looking A.R.P. Warden.

After the tour Robert, John Paul and John Bonham were to take separate vacations with their families.

1979. Knebworth UK. Dramatic photo of Robert onstage before 150,000 people.

natural causes.

A subsequent autopsy proved inconclusive, and in the Daily Express of October 8th Alex Hendry reported that John had died from a massive overdose of vodka and orange on a 12-hour drinking spree. He had drunk so much alcohol — about 40 measures — that

THE DEATH OF JOHN BONHAM

On Thursday, September 25, 1980 John Bonham was found dead at Jimmy's newly acquired home, the Old Mill House in Mill Lane, Windsor — the house Jimmy had purchased from actor Michael Caine for around £900,000 in August.

A first post mortem failed to reveal any obvious cause of death, although suicide was not suspected. It was assumed he died from

his blood alcohol level was at least three-and-half times over the legal limit for drivers.

Pathologist Dr Edmund Hemsted told the inquest at Windsor, Berkshire, that the drink had made John sick, water-logged his lungs, and killed him.

John's chauffeur and personal assistant, Rex King, said the fatal drinking session began at lunchtime on September 24th, in a pub near John's home in Hereford, before they drove to a rehearsal in Windsor.

John had about four or five quadruple measures of vodka and orange in the pub, then carried on drinking at the rehearsal studios, and when they went to Jimmy's home he was downing generous measures of vodka and orange at the rate of two or three drinks an hour.

Around midnight the drummer fell asleep on a sofa, and King and Rick Hobbs, Jimmy Page's personal assistant, carried him upstairs to bed.

Mr Hobbs said that when he put John to bed he laid him on his side and braced him with pillows, for he had "had experience before, of people being drunk".

Six hours later, when the group's road manager, Louis LeFevre, arrived and went to John's room he immediately noticed something wrong. He checked the drummer's pulse, then called a doctor, who pronounced John dead.

Jimmy told East Berkshire coroner, Mr Robert Wilson, that when John arrived at the rehearsal studio he was "pretty tipsy". The coroner recorded a verdict of accidental death.

The tragedy led to speculation about the group's future, and Melody Maker and Record Mirror published tributes from Cozy Powell, Carl Palmer, Stewart Copeland, Phil Collins and B.P. Fallon, in their October 4th issues.

In Record Mirror, Robin Smith wrote: "John Bonham never admitted to being a fancy technician, but played from the bottom of his formidable soul. On vinyl and

Jimmy and Robert in action.

1980. John Paul's 'look' onstage during the "Zeppelin Over Europe" final tour.

onstage he gave everything. His finest and lasting testament will always be the opening thunder of *Rock and Roll.*"

Former Swan Song Vice President, Danny Goldberg, who now heads Modern Records, said in Rolling Stone, "He had this incredible talent. I don't think there's ever been anybody like him. As brilliant as Jimmy Page is, Led Zeppelin will never be the same without John. It may be better, it may be worse. But there's no one else in the world who can play drums like that."

The funeral was held in the parish church near to

Rushock, Worcestershire, not far from the Bonham farm.

Because the band and family wished the ceremony to be conducted with as little publicity as possible, only eight drenched fans stood in the rain on Friday, October 10th, by contrast to the 250 mourners who attended the chapel for the cremation in Worcestershire. Guests from the world of rock music included Roy Wood, Bev Bevan, Jeff Lynne and Denny Laine, as well as John's wife, Pat, and children Jason and Zoe.

The national dailies

were quick to pick up on the possibility of the group splitting, but the music press suggested as possible replacements Aynsley Dunbar, Simon Kirke, Cozy Powell, Peter Criss and Carmine Appice. They bore in mind that Zeppelin had been preparing for a 19-venue North American tour in October, concentrating on local capitals like Dallas and avoiding the major New York-style venues.

Forum Montreal, Canada	Oct 17
Capitol Center Landover, Maryland	Oct 19
Capitol Center Landover, Maryland	Oct 21
Spectrum Philadelphia, Pennsylvania	Oct 22
Capitol Center Landover, Maryland	Oct 23
Richfield Coliseum Cleveland, Ohio	Oct 26
Richfield Coliseum Cleveland, Ohio	Oct 27
Joe Louis Stadium Detroit, Michigan	Oct
Joe Louis Stadium Detroit, Michigan	Oct
War Memorial Auditorium Buffalo, New York	Nov
Spectrum Philadelphia, Pennsylvania	Nov
Spectrum Philadelphia, Pennsylvania	Nov
Civic Arena Pittsburgh, Pennsylvania	Nov
Civic Arena Pittsburgh, Pennsylvania	Nov
Civic Center St. Paul, Minnesota	Nov
Stadium Chicago, Illinois	Nov
Stadium Chicago, Illinois	Nov
Stadium Chicago, Illinois	Nov
Stadium Chicago, Illinois	Nov

But on Thursday, December 4th, Zeppelin and their management made the following announcement in the press: "We wish it to be known that the loss of our dear friend and the deep respect we have for his family, together with the sense of undivided harmony felt by ourselves and our manager, have léd us to decide that we could ot continue as we were." So, to all intents and urposes the group had plit, but speculation bout their individual tures remained. It was ought that Robert, who ad a stockpile of songs, ight pursue a solo career r form a band along the nes of Rockpile (who also plit, soon after Led eppelin).

Jimmy Page was known o be interested in a mass uitar project, changing e actual sounds of usical instruments, and

lifting them out of the musical genres.

The only other possibility that seemed open at the time was that the remaining members would attempt to gauge public reaction to a split, in the anticipation that groundswell opinion would reach such a level that they would have no alternative but to return to the stage.

TRIBUTES

B.P. Fallon, the group's former publicist and personal friend: *"There's so much bullshit in the Fleet Street rags about Led Zeppelin's kharma — Zeppelin have given more pleasure to more millions than possibly any other band in the world.*

"Fragments of memories are burning through my mind, like being at Bonzo's house and his son Jason playing a James Brown record on the juke box, and playing along to it

brilliantly on the small drum kit his father had bought for him. If James Brown had been there he would have been as proud and smiling as Jason's dad.

"Like being in a Lear jet with Zeppelin when Bonzo took it into his head to pilot this small executive rocket. Bits of chicken leg and bottles of champagne swizzling around the tiny cabin as Bonzo looped-the-loop. It was so exhilaratingly terrifying that all we could do was laugh and hang on to our seats, literally!" (Abridged

Top: 1980. Jimmy in shades and wearing one of a succession of suits worn onstage for the final Zeppelin tour, "Zeppelin Over Europe".
Bottom: 1980. John Bonham during Zeppelin's final tour.

ジミー・ペイジ健在！

version of Fallon's tribute, which appeared in *Melody Maker*).

Bob Geldof of the Boomtown Rats: "*John Bonham deserved his place as one of the great British drummers. Without him, Led Zeppelin wouldn't have had the initial success they had so amazingly quickly. His drumming was as noticeable as Page's guitar playing. You* noticed *the drummer. You'd go 'Jesus!' at the drumming — it's just sad.*" (Melody Maker).

Chris Welch of *Musician's Only* magazine and personal friend of the group: "*In the last couple of years John dropped his* Moby Dick *solo and experts felt his drumming was getting crisper. He was bawdy, and liked his beer, but he could take it. He used*

to get very nervous before big concerts and would be sick on the plane on the way — yet he could drum for three hours. I don't think we'll see the likes of him again."

To many fans John's death was like the death of a friend or a relative, and in many cases it was felt to be one of the worst tragedies of rock'n'roll.

Fortunately, the commercial exploitation which occurred after the deaths of Elvis Presley, John Lennon, Marc Bolan, Jimi Hendrix, Brian Jones, and so forth, did not occur in John's case.

Only one American magazine *Led Zeppelin — Will the Song Remain the Same?* dwelt on the subject. Among its articles on the band was one by

Top Left: *1980. "Zeppelin Over Europe".*
Top Right *and* **Bottom:** *Jimmy dispenses with the jacket for the 1980 European summer shows.*

"as tough as Bonham's."

The *Playboy* tribute had the grace to add: "We'll miss the incredible time keeper who could solo for 30 minutes and leave his audience screaming for more."

After the tragic assassination of ex-Beatle John Lennon outside his home in New York in December 1980, it became more difficult to locate the remaining Zeppelin members, who had become more security conscious, but of the "reforming" rumors floating around the strongest originated from the *Los Angeles Times*, which tipped Alan White as drummer, Chris Squire as bassist, with John Paul on keyboards, Jimmy on lead guitar and Robert taking lead vocals. It was stated that no definite name for this line-up had been thought of.

On March 10, 1981 Jimmy made a guest appearance at London's Hammersmith Odeon for an encore of *Goin' Down* with guitarist Jeff Beck.

Robert played small capacity UK dates such as Keele University, and the Blue Note Club in Derby, with the band The Honeydrippers, playing old Elvis Presley, blues numbers and more or less versions of records from his personal collection.

Katherine Luskus who claimed to have charted the careers of almost every major group from Cream to Jethro Tull, and who claimed to have written a letter dated September 19, 1979, detailing "a change in Led Zeppelin's

membership...the change will come under very tragic circumstances."

Playboy magazine published a short tribute, which quoted Jimmy's remarks on encountering John for the first time: "I couldn't believe how he

was living his music. When he gets into a trip, the audience goes with him."

Sometimes John would drum with his hands, which prompted one manufacturer to make the claim that its drums were

1980. All shots from Zeppelin's Japanese tour.

OFFICIAL ZEPPELIN ALBUMS

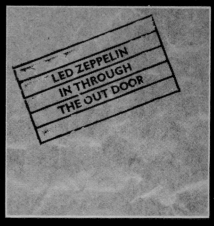

DISCOGRAPHY OF OFFICIAL
UK & USA RELEASES

Albums (UK & USA)

Led Zeppelin (One), ATLANTIC K 40031, 1969
Led Zeppelin II, ATLANTIC K 40037, 1969
Led Zeppelin III, ATLANTIC DE LUXE 2401 002, 1970
Led Zeppelin IV, ("The Four Symbols Album"),
    ATLANTIC K 50008, 1971
Houses of the Holy, ATLANTIC K 50014, 1973
Physical Graffiti (Double), SWAN SONG SSK 89400/A &
    SSK 89400/B, 1975
Presence, SWAN SONG SSK 59402, 1976
The Song Remains the Same (Double; film sound-track),
    SWAN SONG SSK 89402, 1976
In Through the Out Door, SWAN SONG SSK 59410, 1979

Singles (USA only)

Communication Breakdown / Good Times, Bad Times,
    ATLANTIC 2613, 1969
Whole Lotta Love / Livin' Lovin' Maid (She's Just a Woman),
    ATLANTIC 2690, 1969
Immigrant Song / Hey Hey What Can I Do, ATLANTIC 2777, 1970
Black Dog / Misty Mountain Hop, ATLANTIC 2849, 1971
Rock and Roll / Four Sticks, ATLANTIC 2865, 1972
Over the Hills and Far Away / Dancing Days,
    ATLANTIC 2970, 1973
D'Yer Maker / The Crunge, ATLANTIC 2986, 1973
Trampled Underfoot / Black Country Woman,
    SWAN SONG SS 70102, 1975
Candy Store Rock / Royal Orleans, SWAN SONG SS 70110, 1976
Fool in the Rain / Hot Dog, SWAN SONG SS 71003, 1979

Other

The four members of Led Zeppelin are guests on P.J. Proby's
Three Week Hero (Album, LIBERTY LBL 83219E, 1969)

Hey, Hey What Can I Do, released as a single in the USA, features
on the UK album, **New Age of Atlantic** (ATLANTIC 20024, 1972)

Personal Details

JAMES PATRICK PAGE Born January 9, 1944 in Heston, Middlesex.
JOHN BALDWIN (Stage name John Paul Jones) Born January 3, 1946 in Sidcup, Kent.
ROBERT ANTHONY PLANT Born August 20, 1948 in West Bromwich, Staffs.
JOHN HENRY BONHAM Born May 31, 1948 in Redditch, Worcestershire.
Manager PETER GRANT
Quote from Robert Plant to Chris Charlesworth —
"Peter is the fifth member of the group, and as much as we have a highly conscientious attitude about our material…so too has Peter. He's the person with the responsibility on his shoulders, but he's never run us — he's always put things to us for joint decisions."

ACKNOWLEDGEMENTS

Grateful acknowledgement is made to the following journals, corporations and individuals for permission to reproduce photographs used in the preparation of this book — *Creem, Radio Times, Crawdaddy, People Magazine, Proximity, Viva Rock, Music Life, Circus, Atlantic Records Archives, Bill Graham Promotional Posters, Swan Song Records, Uniphoto, Chris Dreja, Norwood Price, John C Rettie, Barry Plummer, Robert Ellis, Ara Ashjiam, Barrie Wentzell, Pennie Smith, Phil Burner, Neil Zlozower, Neal Preston, Stuart G Liben, Matt Susskind, John T Comerford III, Simon Fowler, Kevin Cummins, Bob Gruen, Mike Barich, Don Hawrglak, Michael N Marks, Alan Perry* and *Chris Turner.*

Every effort has been made to trace and to credit copyright holders of the photographs reproduced; apologies are due to those who have proved untraceable or who remain unknown to the compilers.

Front Cover: *Circa 1977. Jimmy Page and Robert Plant on US Tour.*
Back Cover: *August 1979, Knebworth Festival, UK. Top: Robert Plant; Bottom: John Paul Jones; Left: John Bonham; Right: Jimmy Page.*
Title Page (p.3): *Circa 1968. Official photograph.*

Howard Mylett is the world's foremost authority on Led Zeppelin. At the age of seven he became an avid collector of records and books on the groups and artists of the era, and developed a particular fondness for the early recordings of Elvis Presley. This led to a more intensified interest in the music of The Beatles and The Rolling Stones. He worked with **Roy Carr**, Special Projects Editor of New Musical Express, on the compilation of two huge-selling, world-wide editions of The Illustrated Record Book, featuring both these groups. From 1969 he concentrated his attention on the growth of Led Zeppelin. In 1976 his paperback book Led Zeppelin was published, and is now in its third printing. He is 34 and lives in Brighton, England, with his wife. He was educated at Lewes Grammar School where his interest in writing first developed.

25-year-old **Richard Bunton's** interest in Led Zeppelin started in 1970. His musical tastes encompass bands like Van Halen, Montrose, Aerosmith and Queen, but his main attention has been focussed on Led Zeppelin, enabling him to build up a substantial collection of Led Zeppelin material and to develop a thorough knowledge of the band's development and their music. He traveled with the band on their last 'Zeppelin Over Europe' tour. A bookshop manager by profession, he lives in Manchester, England.